CONFESSIONS OF A BOSS MOM

CONFESSIONS

—— OF A ——

BOSS MOM

The Power In Knowing We Are Not Alone

DANA MALSTAFF

Disclaimer: This book is not intended as a substitute for the medical advice of physicians. The reader should regularly consult a physician in matters relating to his/her health and particularly with respect to any symptoms that may require diagnosis or medical attention. All of the opinions expressed in this book are that of the author, and are only meant to be just that, an opinion. The Author and Publisher assumes or undertakes NO LIABILITY for any loss or damage suffered as a result of the use, misuse or reliance on the information provided in this book.

The fact that an organization or website is referred to in this work as citation or a potential source of further information does not mean that the Author or Publisher endorses the recommendations that it may make.

Readers should be aware that Internet websites listed in this work may have changed or disappeared between when this work was written and when it is read.

Cover Design: Lilah Higgins of Higgins Creative
www.waketomake.com
Interior Design: Alexa Bigwarfe of Write.Publish.Sell
www.writepublishsell.co
Editing: Liz Thompson
Author Photo: C.J. Thomas, cjthomasphotography.com

Published by Kat Biggie Press.

ISBN-13: 978-0-9987779-3-1
Library of Congress Control Number: 2017
First Edition: July 2017

10 9 8 7 6 5 4 3 2 1

Dedication

To every Boss Mom in the world. Thank you for showing your children that pursuing your passion is important. I know the journey can be tough, but you are not alone.

And to Emily Potts, a beautiful Boss Mom who gave so much love to this world. You will never be forgotten, and you will always be cherished.

CONTENTS

A Note to the Reader

In case someone hasn't told you lately, you are pretty awesome. I might not know you, but I know this is true because, like all Boss Moms, you are trying to create a beautiful world in which you are proud to live. You are constantly faced with challenges and every single day you decide to keep moving forward. I want you to know that you are in the right place.

I know being a Boss Mom is hard. Being a mom or an entrepreneur all by herself is ridiculously challenging, and I know that there has been more than one occasion where you might have questioned yourself. For me, there has been more than one occasion, in fact too many instances to count, when I have felt inadequate as a mom, a wife, a daughter, an employee, an entrepreneur, and pretty much everything else under the sun. We all question how we live our lives at some point, but it doesn't have to be that way.

I look at my children and am envious that they don't know about judgment, hatred, loss, embarrassment, or fear. They are curious and bold, and I hope every day that they can keep their childlike wonder for the rest of their lives.

This book isn't about some confession we make because we feel guilty, this book is about a bold proclamation that we refuse to feel guilty about our choices any longer.

This book is about realizing that we are all living in the same world, trying to figure it all out. This book is about acceptance, empathy, connection, and love. Yes, we dive into the world of being a Boss Mom, but no matter who you are, or where you came from, I think you will find that this book is an open door to a better world. So let's hold hands and step through that door together.

A Special Invitation

Here at Boss Mom, our motto is, 'no judgment, just dance parties.' We know that we are all so different and yet we are all the same. We know that in each stage of being a woman, a mom, and an entrepreneur, that we are faced with times of guilt, and we are here to tell you that you should shed that guilt right now. You heard me, throw that guilt away because no one is perfect, and the more you try, the harder it gets. What you need, what we all need, is a safe place where women will offer up ideas and support without the judgment. A place where we feel connected, loved and accepted. A place where we challenged to be ourselves instead of sacrifice ourselves. And that is how the amazing Boss Mom Movement and community was started. I created the Boss Mom Movement because I needed this kind of place and couldn't find it.

The Boss Mom Movement was born in 2015 when the first Boss Mom book was published, and it sprung forth a movement that is all about being real and authentic about the challenges of being a parent and an entrepreneur. We believe that the more you share your experiences, the more you will see that you are not alone. And even with the challenges we face, we believe that life can be joyous and we seek to celebrate those moments together (sometimes with a dance party).

If this sounds like your kind of place, then join us at www.boss-mom.com You can hop into our Facebook Group at www.boss-mom.com/facebook.

I can't wait to see you there,
Dana Malstaff CEO, Boss Mom LLC

ps. If you want help finding the right communities for you then make sure to grab my free Boss Mom Companion course. I walk you through a proven process to help you find and engage with the right communities. Grab it for free at www.boss-mom.com/bmc

Part 1:

NO ONE CAN EVER PREPARE YOU

THE TRUTH ABOUT TRUTHS

Today you received a piece of advice. Someone at some point today approached you and told you something that they sincerely believed was important and true. They probably gave you this advice because they care about you and thought that it would be helpful. It was all done with good intentions, but sometimes good intentions end with stress, frustrations, questions, and tears.

So what was this advice? Well, it depends. I think to get to the bottom of this we need to back up a little.

Every day you have new experiences. From the moment you are born you begin to see and understand the world in a particular way. Certain expectations are set by your family, teachers, and friends. As you grow up, some of these expectations and perceptions are shifted, and some become even more deep-rooted. The way you have come to understand the world and how it works that seems completely real and true to you. And it is.

Each one of us goes through life with our own set of truths that we carry with us. When we meet someone who looks like they are having, or about to have, a similar experience that we have had then we pull out our bag of truths and look to see if there is some bit of advice we can offer up to help.

Most of us come from a place of support when we offer advice, but we don't always realize that no matter how similar our experiences might be, we are always different.

Now, it's important to mention that sometimes we get advice that is right in line with who we are and what we are experiencing, and our lives are forever changed. This is the sole reason why we must never stop sharing our experiences and truths with the world.

The challenge arises when someone is so persistent about their truth that it begins to weigh on you like a lead brick stuck to your feet dragging you down to the bottom of the river. Sometimes someone else's truth can make your life harder, and who wants that?

Or, more commonly, many people come to you with that same truth that you start to question yourself and wonder if that particular piece of advice must be a universal truth.

I am here to tell you that TRENDS ARE NOT UNIVERSAL TRUTHS.

I'll give you two common examples: Everyone should go to college, and if you can be a parent you should have children.

These two examples are the opinion of a lot of people, but not ALL people. These two topics have sparked many heated debates and probably ruined a number of relationships. We are often passionate about our truths, but that does not mean that everyone in the world has to follow your path. In fact, it is quite the contrary.

For me, I started to realize that some of my perceptions of the world were different than the trend when I was pregnant with my son. I am a firm believer that positive energy is important, and I wanted to create a positive and stress-free space for him when he was born.

When I found out I was pregnant, I did some research and discovered a concept called hypnobirthing that was all about the idea that we accentuate the pain of birth by being scared and stressed during labor. The idea is that if we can shift our mindset to understand that childbirth is a natural process that was not meant to be painful, then we can reduce the pain. I remember being so excited about the idea and I immediately got the books and the tapes and began to learn everything I could about the practice.

The funny thing was that every time I would mention it to someone they almost always talked about how having a baby was painful and it was silly for me to think otherwise. They would talk about their terrible birthing experience and how I should prepare myself.

I know that they were just trying to be helpful, but in all honesty, it wasn't helpful. Their good intentions caused a lot of unneeded stress and anxiety. Why were they so compelled to force their truth on me? I can only imagine that a hard labor would burn a vibrant memory in your brain that made the idea of a calm and pain-free labor sound impossible. But still, while their advice came from a good place, it was unsolicited, and it was given to contradict the truth I wanted to create for myself.

I think that all pieces of advice should be followed up with something like, "that is how I experienced it, and I know that we all experience things differently, so I hope everything goes just as you planned."

This book is all about honoring each other's truths, and not feeling guilty when our truths are different from one another.

Oh the Guilt

No one ever told me I would feel horribly guilty that I wanted my kids to take a nap so I could work on my business. No one told me that I would question my ability to be a good mother because I didn't want to be with my kids 24/7. And no one ever told me how alone I would feel, wondering if I was the only one feeling this way.

It turns out there is a lot of guilt involved in creating and growing babies and businesses.

Before you embark on the journey to become a parent, you are mainly freaked out trying to figure out how on earth you will find the time to raise a baby when you already feel like there isn't enough time in the day to get everything done.

Most of us spent time reading about how to have a smooth pregnancy, how to not go crazy from all the hormones pumping through our bodies, and what size fruit our babies were that week.

I do remember being worried that I might not be a great mom, but I didn't know what that really meant.

Then my son was born, and it was a whole new world of guilt. I loved him, but I wasn't in love with him at first. I breastfed, but I mainly cried all the time because it was so hard, I wanted him to take naps so I could work on my new business website. All of this, and so much more contributed to a constant feeling of guilt that I just wasn't cut out to be a good mom. Or even worse, that I could be a great mom if I were just more dedicated to my child.

But it was all a bunch of bologna.

I see now that if you care enough about your children to worry if you are being a good mom, then you are a good mom. And let's

be honest, there are no perfect moms so let's stop trying to be perfect.

I see now that I felt guilty because I wasn't confident in my decisions as a parent yet, and that is a completely normal feeling.

I see now that I was not the only one who felt guilty, nor was I the only one who is not cut out to be a stay-at-home mom, but am still a good mom.

I see now that thousands and thousands of women feel exactly the way I felt. It feels so good to know I am not alone, and right about now you should be feeling pretty good too.

Cut yourself some slack and take a deep breath. We all feel guilty sometimes, it's inevitable. We feel guilty about different things, but it happens to us all.

You are so not alone! Now, I don't think that knowing you are not alone will solve all of your guilt problems, but I think it helps.

If you want to get rid of your guilt altogether, then I am sad to say that I don't have a silver bullet solution for you. I think that we all question our decisions and stress out about the responsibility of being a parent and having our own business because we care. When you care about something, then you want it to flourish, and that means that if you don't do your job correctly that thing you love might not make it in this world. The responsibility you feel is normal, in fact, I think it's healthy to a certain extent. Let's just not let that guilt weigh us down so much.

Feeling guilty doesn't serve you, and it just eats up your energy, and as Boss Moms we are tired enough as it is.

Here is my solution for feeling guilty: Start accepting your decisions and stop worrying so much about whether you are doing it right. Accept that 'right' is a matter of opinion and your opinion is the one that matters when it comes to your family and business. Of course, you should try to educate yourself on how to parent when you feel like you need extra support, and accept advice as it comes, but always listen to your inner voice that tells you what's right for you. You can challenge yourself to always work to be a better parent and entrepreneur, but never let anyone make you feel like you are a bad parent because that just isn't true.

We will talk more about this whole guilt epidemic a bit later, but for now, sit back and know that you are in a safe place and I already know that you are a beautiful light in this world and I am sure glad you are here.

The Reality about Judgment

We are all judgmental. I don't think we can help it. I mean if we all have our own truths that shape how we see the world, and we know that other people have different beliefs systems that we don't understand, then judgment is inevitable.

I guess the question is whether or not judgment is a bad thing. I like the phrase 'everything in moderation.' Judgement can help us gain clarity on what we truly care about and are willing to fight for. I think judgment can help us assess our surroundings and sometimes protects us. **But mostly, I think judgment is a reflex that needs to be managed and is usually an incorrect assessment.**

How many times have you found yourself in the grocery store and seen someone pass by that was wearing a low-cut shirt, looked wrinkled and disheveled, or well-put-together and the first thing you do is sum up who they are right then and there?

I have done it, and I still do it. I can't help myself.

Now maybe if you are The Mentalist or that guy from the Liar Liar Show, then you might be able to read people accurately, but I can't. We are culturally conditioned to believe that women who wear low-cut tops are slutty, people who wear wrinkled clothes must not care or be that smart, and that people that are too well-put-together are prissy and full of themselves. Are these true statements? Probably some of the time, but not all of the time. And what if the woman in that low-cut shirt finally got a night out after being on pm duty for a month straight and wanted to feel like a woman again. And that guy with the wrinkled shirt did a 12-hour shift and threw on clothes because he realized he didn't have food in the house and had to be back at work in the morning. And maybe that prissy looking woman works ridiculous hours and cries in the car because she missed her daughter's first steps. The point is that no scientist would ever publish a conclusion from one sampling, and neither should we.

The bummer is that there are a lot of people that make decisions about who you are right when they meet you, and it's really hard to change their mind.

There are times when I have felt judged (I think we all have felt judged at one point or another) but I didn't really begin to feel it strongly until I became a mom and an entrepreneur.

I felt judged for deciding to start my own business.

I felt judged for deciding to have my kids naturally.

I felt judged for breastfeeding my son in public.

I could go on and on, and I bet you are thinking about all the ways that you felt judged on your Boss Mom journey.

Maybe you felt judged for deciding to have only one child, or for having more than three.

Maybe you felt judged for getting divorced or not getting married at all.

Maybe you felt judged for deciding not to breastfeed or for asking the nurse for an epidural.

The funny part about judgment is that it is all around us, all the time. Just as we are feeling judged, we are judging others because we are all different people with different truths and we just can't help ourselves.

Judgment is a perpetual cycle of misunderstanding other people's truths and decisions. I mean, if judgment were sound waves that you could see, then the air would be so thick that we wouldn't be able to move around half the time. We would be stuck, standing still, and that is just what judgment does, it paralyzes us.

We feel paralyzed by judgment because it makes us question, and feel guilty about, our decisions. You begin to feel like you have to explain yourself and why you do the things you do, but no explanation is needed.

So what is the solution? You are!

The next time you make a judgment about someone else, stop for a minute and remember that you are only catching a glimpse into that person's life. They have a much bigger story to tell, and our lives would all be better if we spent a little more time getting to know each other.

THE LOVE AT FIRST SIGHT MYTH

Did you know that the moment you meet your baby, you will fall into a deep, timeless love that will last forever? That is what they told me. So when my son was born, and I didn't feel that endless love I thought something must be wrong with me.

It would only be much later, before my second child, that I would come out and say that it was not love at first sight when my baby was born. And I think, even though I don't have official statistics on this, that there is a fair share of women out there that had the same experience.

I mean, let's be honest. You just spent nine months in a total state of the unknown with hormonal chaos, feeling uncomfortable, a looming feeling that you will never get to be the true you again, and that you will now be required to sacrifice it all for your child. You then spend hours and hours (maybe more) pushing and breathing, and after complete exhaustion sets in, a little baby pops out and is placed on your chest, and that's if you have textbook labor. You, my friend, are in shock. A LOT has happened in a short amount of time; even though it probably felt like an eternity. Don't get me wrong, you are happy. You are full of joy and excitement, but love, maybe not.

Now you might be shaking your head saying that you fell in love right from the start and that's cool too, but for a lot of us, we feel pretty bad about not being in love with our babies when they are born.

Please don't feel bad.

When you met your partner, did you know right that very second that you were in love? Probably not. In fact, if you met someone and took them home to your family and said it was love and you were moving in together that very moment, everyone would tell you that you are crazy and to rethink your decision.

Having a baby is no different. Love can take time to grow, and it might take longer for some than others.

You may think that because you grew that baby in your belly that you know each other, but you don't. There is an insane bond there that you can't explain for sure, but it takes time to get to know each other. Allow yourself the time and space to fall in love.

And the myth that one must fall in love at first sight doesn't just apply to when you give birth; it also applies to the birth and creation of your business. You might have an idea that you love, but the process of starting and growing a business is hard, and it will take time for your idea to really settle in. The relationship you have with your business will have ups and downs just like any relationship you will ever have, and that includes the relationship with yourself.

Once you fall in love, though, you will always love your kids and your business. But let's be brutally honest, loving someone and being in love are not the same thing. Feeling love for your kids and business is all about wanting them to thrive, but being in love means you are passionate about being with them as much as possible, and there are many times when we want to get away from our kids and our businesses.

If you are in love with your business, but it isn't loving you back and just isn't working then take a step back and see if it is really a two-way relationship.

No matter what situation you are in right now, remember that love is fluid and it takes work from both sides. Falling in love takes time, so if it's taking more time than you would like, or you are working on falling back in love with your babies or business, give yourself some grace. There are a lot of us that are right there with you.

THE GLORIFIED HUSTLE

I'm a hustler. I work hard because that's what moms and entrepreneurs do. Wait, that doesn't sound fair, or fun.

Have you ever looked up the definition of 'hustle'?

When used as a verb, hustle means "to force (someone) to move hurriedly or unceremoniously in a specified direction." And as a noun, it either means "busy movement and activity," or to "swindle."

The word 'unceremoniously' means that when you hustle you are being pushed without courtesy or respect. I don't know about you, but neither of those definitions sounds like something I should be proud of, so how did this term become a badge of pride?

A whole lot of us moms and entrepreneurs feel like it's a rite of passage to be exhausted and lost most of the time. That is one of those 'trendy truths' that is passed down to you as soon as you become a mom or an entrepreneur.

"It's going to be hard, and you are going to have to make sacrifices, so get ready." That is what we hear, right?

Well, I am not here to tell you that statement is incorrect. I have experienced both challenges and sacrifices being a mom and being an entrepreneur, and I can tell you that it's hard, but I think we are approaching it the wrong way.

Just because something is hard, doesn't mean we have to sacrifice ourselves to make it work. We might have seasons of hustle when we are launching a product, or potty training our child, but to live in a constant state of hustle for our children or businesses is unhealthy and unnecessary.

So why do we wear our 'hustle' like a badge of honor? Why do we create hustle hashtags and wear shirts about how hard we hustle? I know I used to be that way and I loved talking about how I was living the dream and hustling hard.

But then I met Lara McCulloch, and it shifted my mindset about how I hustle. At the time, she was doing a "Boycott the Hustle" campaign, and she made me realize how much I was using the word 'hustle' in my daily talk. She made me realize that I was using the word 'hustle' to justify why I was tired and irritable. I was letting the word 'hustle' become an excuse for why I was always behind on work, why I made a mistake, or why I was late to a call.

Don't get me wrong, there is a time and a place to hustle, but we should not glorify the idea of the long-term hustle as if it is some requirement to be successful because that just isn't true. We are behind on work or late to a meeting because we didn't manage our time for that day, or overcommitted with a client. Maybe our kid got sick, or we got sick, and that caused us to fall behind on our work, but those things are just events that happen in our lives, and since we know there will be a certain amount of these unexpected events in our lives then we can begin to build a cushion into our schedule. And when something big happens and throws us off our center, then we can have a finite time when we truly hustle, but I believe we should stop glorifying the word 'hustle' because it does not serve us in any positive way.

My desire is to give you space and permission to question whether your hustle is a requirement to being successful and be open to the idea that maybe there is a different way, a more purposeful and strategic way. I truly believe that we can accomplish so much in this world while having thriving families and careers without burning ourselves out and it starts with believing that a thriving life is possible.

SELF-SELECTED ISOLATION

I was about to leave for Las Vegas on our very first no-kids weekend in three years when I realized I had forgotten to drop the kid's lunches off at school. My mom was driving me to the airport and got to witness me freak out as I frantically called daycare and embarrassingly ask them to feed my children. I got off the phone and mentioned that I bet I was the first parent to forget their kid's lunch.

My mom said something I will never forget: "How snooty of you to think that you are the ONLY mom to every forget your kid's lunch."

WOW! I had never thought about it that way. I voluntarily isolated myself and made statements that made me feel like I must be a bad parent that made mistakes that no one else would make. But my mom made me realize that every parent forgets things and every parent makes mistakes.

A few months later, I was dropping my kids off at school, and a dad came in and said: "Shoot! I forgot my daughter's lunch again, can you feed her and put it on my bill?" He said it without guilt, and the ladies smiled and nodded, and he left.

Ah ha! I wasn't the only one, and neither are you.

We feel alone because we don't share our experiences, both good and bad. We get scared that we will be judged or find out that we are a bad parent or not cut out to be an entrepreneur.

But if I were going to claim one universal truth, this is it: "The more we share and connect, the more we accept."

Share your story, share your challenges, share the messy parts of your life because if you don't then you might end up going through life feeling unnecessarily guilty, and no one wants that. In fact, I bet there are ladies in our Boss Mom group at this very moment that feel the same way you do and want to connect and share their story with you.

The more we share our stories, the more we can see that we are not alone, that we are all imperfect and that it's ok. We can all learn from each other without judgment, and I believe the world is a better place when we connect and support one another.

Part 2:

WE ARE ALL DIFFERENT AND YET ALL THE SAME

COMMON GROUND

I like to think of experiences as puzzle pieces. The manufacturer mass produces each piece and then adds them to the appropriate puzzle. Each of our lives is a unique combination of puzzle pieces, but we always have some pieces in common.

Even though the picture that our puzzle creates looks different from each other, we still share common pieces. When we go out into the world and try to connect, we often try to find people that have the most pieces in common with us, but what if I told you that you only needed to have one piece in common to create a strong connection with someone?

I know that we all want to find our tribe and connect with people that really 'get' us, but you are a dynamic lady made up of many puzzle pieces, which means finding someone that 'gets' you can mean a lot of things. You and your partner might have a similar sense of humor and a similar love of adventure. You and your best friend might connect when it comes to talking about business, and you might have a group of friends from college that you connect through your past experiences. Who knows, you might have someone in your life that you just love, but have no idea why you feel a connection because you are so different. The main thing to remember is that **you don't have to have everything in common to share common ground.**

When you reach out to connect with other women about your current challenges, know that they might have experienced it the same, similarly, or differently than you, and that's ok. It is important to acknowledge that others have shared similar challenges as us, even if their outcome or advice is not the same. The point is not that we all have the same experience; the point is that we see that we are not the only one having that kind of experience. Knowing that we are not alone is often the push we need to open up about our experiences and get support and give support and that kind of community changes lives.

Now, my life has resulted in one kind of journey, and if I were to only talk about my journey and no one else's, then it would only resonate with women who have shared my struggles and successes. I want each and every woman to know that no matter what you are going through, there are women out there sharing the same struggles. Yes, you guessed it, you are not alone. There is no need to continue crying on the bathroom floor feeling like you are on an island.

No one should have to feel guilty or alone and, if you do, you don't have to anymore. Throughout, this book, I will share powerful stories of women who have experienced a vast array of struggles as moms and entrepreneurs.

Remember that this book is about not feeling alone, so naturally, we are going to focus on the struggles that women experience in different areas of our lives. Our goal is, to be honest about how women of all backgrounds and circumstances feel in different situations, and how we realize we need support and how to find it. I believe that being transparent and honest about how we feel is not only uplifting for others but also therapeutic for ourselves.

Each woman in this book, and thousands upon thousands more, have a unique story, that is important and valid. Your story is important and should be shared, not just to help others, but to help yourself. When you keep your hardships bottled up inside, they create pressure and stress until one day they erupt like a volcano of sadness and anger.

If you think that no one wants to hear your story, then you are wrong. Your story might just be the thing that changes someone's life. And one of these women's stories might be the one that changes your life, so open your heart and get ready to hear amazing stories from wonderful women just like you.

All Kinds of Labels

When we become parents, we don't realize that we have just earned a label. Yep, we are now a 'mom,' and that will most likely be the first thing you tell people from here on out, but that is not the only label you will ever have. Depending on your unique situation, you might have self-imposed labels, or find yourself being labeled against your will. In some ways, our labels help us connect and find each other, but they can also create judgment or assumptions that cause us to tear down relationships instead of building them.

These stories do not represent every possible situation; they are only a glimpse into different women's lives. I encourage you to read each story even if you don't think you can identify with that experience because a broadened understanding of how other people feel and experience various situations will grow the empathy muscle we all need to work every day.

Work-at-Home Mom

I was never built to be a stay-at-home mom. I think I always knew that, but when I got pregnant with my son, I wasn't sure what to expect. I kept telling myself that I should want to stay home with my baby or everyone would think I was a terrible mom. I had quit my job to try to make it on my own and had instantaneously gotten pregnant. I spent nine months trying to make a brand-new business work before my whole world got turned upside down. Once my son was born, I felt completely divided between wanting to be with him and wanting him to take a nap so I could work.

My son was a textbook pregnancy, and he was born healthy and happy, which made me feel like I had nothing to complain about and just needed to suck it up and be happy. Don't get me wrong, there were times when I was blissfully content, but a lot of the time I questioned my parenting decisions and had no idea what kind of business I was really building.

When my son was a few months old, I started putting him in daycare for a day or two a week, so I could get some work done. At the time, I wasn't really making any money so paying money so I could be at home and try to make money made me feel inadequate and often made me feel like I had to make it up to my husband for believing in me. I would try to clean more, or cook more to show that I added value in the household. My husband never asked me for these things, but he did ask about my business and gently questioned when I would start making money. My answer was always that it was just around the corner, but that date kept getting pushed out.

One day, I was sitting in a coffee shop while my son was at daycare and I saw two women and a baby sitting close by. It was a mother, grandmother, and grandchild. I began to cry thinking about how hard this all felt and how much I missed my mom. I decided I wanted to move back to California where a lot of my family lived. Since it was the middle of winter and in the negative degrees, it was not hard to convince my husband. We prepped our house and put it on the market, packed up our things and moved into a small apartment in San Diego. This is when we decided that we would put our son in full-time daycare and I would really try to make my business work. He was in daycare for three days when I pulled him out because the place just didn't feel right. It took me another few months with him at home and me trying to get work done before I would find him the right learning center.

With my son gone all day, I could finally get some work done, but I had to get serious about what business I was trying to build. I remember when I was living in Columbus that I didn't have any friends that owed their own business and I often felt judged that I was working at home but sending my son away. Looking back, I can't recall with certainty that people were vocally judging me; it might have been that I felt judged, but either way it was very real to me.

A few months after we moved to San Diego, I started attending entrepreneur networking meetings where I found all sorts of women who were doing exactly what I was doing. They were trying to build a business and raise kids at the same time. I began to see that I was not alone and was not weird or insane for doing what I was doing. It reinvigorated me to keep going. I started co-hosting a 'Live Your Legend' meeting—an entrepreneur support group— each month near my house and started to meet more amazing people, but not many of them were moms. It was almost another year before I would decide to write the Boss Mom book and start to build a mom entrepreneur support system.

My biggest advice to any woman who considers herself a Work-at-Home Mom is to counter your own inner critic by joining communities that make you feel less crazy. Find women and entrepreneurs that understand and support you. Make sure you give yourself some grace when it comes to sick kids or business setbacks. Sometimes business will take precedence over family time and sometimes you will drop everything for your family. Don't feel guilty about loving your business and only work with people who give you extra space when your kids need you most. If you need support on how to really rock business and babies, then you can read my first book Boss Mom. Until then, we are here to support you every step of the way.

– Dana Malstaff

Single Mom

I have pretty much been a single mom since I got pregnant but still managed to meet someone and fall in love. When my daughter was two, I got engaged and within four months broke off the engagement, had my hours reduced at my teaching job, lost my health insurance benefits, moved, became a single mom again, and then got news that I would be losing my job altogether.

I don't have a Ph.D. I only have a master's degree, which suddenly made me undesirable in my academic position. In the midst of all this, I had started a freelance writing business. Little did I know that business would be the only thing that held me together through all the chaos. It was supposed to be my side hustle, but it became my lifeline.

There was not much in my life that stayed the same or remained stable. Although my paycheck at my teaching job wasn't making me rich, it was always enough, and it was steady. And I was about to lose it entirely. The only constant in my life was my then three-year-old daughter. Whenever someone asks "what's your why?" my answer is her.

When I decided it was best for me to leave my relationship and move out, I was worried about how it would affect my daughter. When I found out I was losing my health insurance, I was worried about how it would affect her. Getting the news that I was about to become unemployed obviously made me worry about how it would affect her.

My teaching job afforded me a lot of flexibility and substantial time off. I only taught on campus three days a week, which meant I was still home with my daughter every other day and every weekend. I had a month off at Christmas and considerable time off from work in the summer months. No other job would pay me well AND give me that kind of time off. I was faced with the prospect of getting a job that paid enough to cover full-time daycare and would keep me away from home and my daughter a lot more than either of us were used to. And that broke my heart. My other option, of course, was to amp up my business. I had previously planned to slowly nurture and grow my business over the next year or so and then take the leap to full-time business owner.

I cried a lot. Then I put my big girl pants (okay, leggings) on and decided to do everything I possibly could to get my business up and running. Being the recovering academic I am, my first line of action was to start researching. I read everything Google could conjure up to learn about the freelance writing world. I read blogs and articles, I followed various successful writers on social media, I subscribed to a ton of newsletters, and I downloaded all pf the freebies I could find. Then I started joining and engaging in some Facebook groups. Whenever I could wake up before my daughter, during naptime, or after bed, I worked at learning about business and worked on becoming more visible to my ideal clients.

Building a life I love for my daughter has always been my #1 motivation. I want to love my life so I can be a happy, engaged and present mom. I want to model what it looks like to dream big and work to make that kind of life. Because if my daughter is ever faced with the decision of working at a job that doesn't bring her joy, or taking a risk on herself to build a life she adores, I hope she always chooses the latter.

My daughter is often involved in my business life, which I love! She ends up hopping on client calls with me occasionally, asks about the women I'm collaborating with and does a happy dance with me whenever I sign a new client! The other day I told her I had something exciting to tell her and she asked, "Did you get a new client!?" (She was equally elated to know that the surprise was actually a trip to our favorite gelato place.)

The wealth of knowledge I gained since entering this entrepreneurial world is astounding. I mean, I knew that the internet was a vast place, but there's this whole world I had no idea was full of opportunities! And honestly, it's full of people that value and support me and my talents. I also learned to have a whole new level of faith. Sometimes even when people around you support you, you're making money, and you enjoy what you do, even then it can be scary to make the decision to strike out on your own. (Because, what if it just stops and goes away at any given moment!?! AHHH!!) That's where faith needs to kick in and lead doubt out the door.

For anyone that finds themselves in a position in which their options are "believe in yourself" or "do the normal thing," ALWAYS bet on yourself. You might be surprised at how many people place their bets in your favor too once you take that chance.

– Tara Bosler

Step-Mom

I was a single mom for ten years. I had married and divorced young but was educated and driven to succeed in the corporate world. I had worked my way up into management early in my career and was determined to climb the proverbial ladder and shatter all the glass ceilings. I loved my life and loved being a single mom to one adorable little boy. I had no interest in remarrying, having more children, or being a stay-at-home mom.

But then I met Steve, my husband, and he was charming, funny, and supportive (and really cute, too). We dated for a few years and then decided to get married. Did I mention that he has four children? Yup! FOUR MORE kids were coming into my life, but I was still working in my corporate job—although a bit less enthusiastically at this point.

Steve and I, having full custody of his children, had to make a decision about how we were going to care for the kids and successfully blend our family, and decided that I would stay home and be a full-time mom and stepmom. End of story, right? Nope. Within months I was beyond frustrated with the stay-at-home mom life. I loved my new family, and in many ways, they enhanced my life, but the stay-at-home mom routine wasn't for me. I needed more. I needed to feel intellectually stimulated. This was never my plan. Why did I give up a six-figure income to stay home and clean toilets and do endless loads of laundry? It was a difficult adjustment to go from a management position where I had a staff, and my opinion and thoughts mattered, to a mom that 'just' takes care of everything that everyone takes for granted. It felt like my life had been hijacked and I was no longer myself. I was losing myself and becoming a stressed out, unhappy, nagging, crazy lady. I did what I felt I had to do to make our new blended family work but at the expense of my identity. I ignored what I knew I needed and wanted, and created a situation where I was resentful of Steve and the kids—through no fault of their own. That's when I decided I needed a lifeline. I started my editing business, House Style Editing, and connected with a community of Boss Moms that understood and supported me.

Steve is a successful executive, and we could afford to hire help with the house and kids, and was able to start a business without financial stress. I am incredibly lucky in that respect. I had the financial freedom to pursue my business and get the coaching I needed to do it right.

Once I got started, I loved that I was not only using my education but was actually earning money doing something I enjoyed and was good at. It had been a long time since I was passionate about work.

My advice for those of you whose parenting journey was not what you planned, don't fall into the trap of giving up on everything you want, care about, have a passion for, and dream to do because life threw you a curveball. My 'becoming a parent' journey is not traditional but four kids came into my life at once, and I did what was necessary to step in and be a mom to them. I cherish my role as a wife, mom, and stepmom, but being a Boss Mom with a thriving business is also an integral part of my life. As a parent, a certain degree of sacrifice is necessary but not to the extent that you lose yourself and become resentful. And, not every family is the picture-perfect family—we all have unique stories and struggles. Embrace your conventional or non-conventional family and find a balance that works for you.

– Liz Thompson

Military Spouse

In 2014, when my husband deployed to Qatar, it was the hardest year of my life. But, it was also the year that I discovered the entrepreneur in me. I started my blog Dog Tags & Heels, mostly as an outlet to be creative and share my life experiences as a military spouse, and more specifically, how to bloom where you are planted. I had no idea the opportunities that lied ahead in the blogging world. I dove in and learned how to generate revenue from freelance writing and affiliate programs.

Then, when my husband came home in August of 2015, and we moved from Ohio to Maryland. I decided to hit the workforce. I applied and interviewed to so many places, only to be disappointed and deflated. Finding employment as a military spouse can be so discouraging. The constant emails and phone calls saying I was over qualified, under qualified, too much experience or not enough experience, the list goes on and on. As a result, and out of frustration, I decided to take another bold step and start my own business.

I went to school for Mass Communications and PR but I had dedicated myself to being a stay-at-home mom, so I never got a chance to use my degree. With my youngest starting Pre-K, I saw an opportunity to spread my entrepreneur wings.

As an entrepreneur, so many things were and still are challenging for me—like delegating. I discovered that I was going to have to learn to delegate at home. Me trying to do everything and build a business was just not doable. I could no longer make the gourmet meals, meal prep, and make homemade granola bars. I went from a full-time stay-at-home mom to work-at-home mom entrepreneur. Everyone in my home was so used to relying on me to do everything—have the fridge stocked, bills paid, and laundry done. I was running myself into the ground, and our routine had to change. We now all share daily and weekly chores. Everyone pitches in and I don't feel the pressure to be all things to everyone all the time.

Ultimately, I think that many military spouses in my situation become discouraged, hurt, and neglected because their husband's career takes priority over their careers, needs, and life desires. Many spouses become complacent, just like I did. My advice is to make your passion a priority.

During a transition everything seems hard but, with time and effort, it will fall into place. And beneath it all, you will find a woman waiting to be discovered, beautiful and eager to share her talent with the world. You don't have to be perfect, spend a lot of money, or build a huge business, start small and build from there. If you focus and work hard, it will happen, and you will be astonished at what you can become.

– Monika Jefferson

Adoption

I never set out to start my own business. I had a long career as a successful high school theater director. I had a great job, working with great students. But then one day my husband's biological clock started ticking, and we decided to adopt a baby girl from China. After we had brought our daughter home, my husband left teaching and became a stay-at-home dad.

About two years later we adopted a baby boy from the Democratic Republic of Congo. A year later we decided to adopt two more boys from Congo. By now we had tapped out all of our savings and our retirement funds, and we still didn't have our boys home yet. But we absolutely knew that our family was not complete, so we started fundraising. We sold everything in our house that wasn't nailed down. We printed T-shirts with the slogan "More Love" printed on them. But holy smokes, adoption is expensive! So I came up with the idea of making blankets out of African Wax Print fabrics and selling them to raise money to bring our boys home. And sales were great! We brought our boys home and settled in as a family of six.

But still, we weren't finished.

We started the process to adopt two more girls from Congo. I know, I know, it sounds crazy! I returned to my blanket sales, but this time I opened an Etsy shop and started my business for real. After a few months of opening the shop, people started contacting me asking if they could buy my fabric instead of the things I was making. I realized it was a heck of a lot easier to cut a yard of fabric and throw it in an envelope than it was to make a blanket. I completely changed the focus of my shop, stocked it with as many African Wax Print fabrics as I could get my hands on, and dove in head first to More Love Mama Global Textiles and Gifts.

Juggling is hard, believe me, I know. We are now a family of eight. Having six kids is insane. I am still a full-time high school teacher. My husband still stays home with all six kids. But now my shop is bigger and better than ever. Which is wonderful and amazing, but some days it is overwhelming. I come home every day from school and work another 3 to 4 hours each evening. My weekends often include another full day of work. My business does not make enough to support my family (having to insure eight people will probably always keep me tied to a "regular" job), but it makes enough to make it worth staying open.

My motivation is my family. I still day dream EVERY DAY that I just might have a breakthrough and be able to do be a full-time entrepreneur. But even if that doesn't happen, my shop may be something that will help me kick-start my retirement from teaching. I started my family late in life, so my kids are still young, but I have a relatively short time left until I can qualify for retirement. I can see myself running this fabric shop for years to come and possibly even passing it on to my kids if any of them are interested. Either way, I am so happy that my side business helped us complete our family.

– Carrie Wood

* * * *

I just love how each of these women has figured out how to make it all work for them in their current situation. We all have different ways we tackle our lives, family, and business but we do what we think is best. No matter what your situation, there is strength in these stories that you can take with you and carry you forward. Remember that you are a beautiful light in this world and your story will help you shine. Don't hide your challenges or feelings, they are part of your story and letting them out into the world will help you see that they don't define you.

Hormones

We all have them. You can't see them so sometimes it's hard to know if they are the cause of that outburst or day of utter despair, but they are there, and they are real.

We all experience hormone imbalances in different ways and for different reasons. While I don't feel like we should use them as an excuse when we dish out less than stellar behavior, sometimes they influence us to act in ways in which we are less than proud.

If you have noticed chronic issues that are possibly related to hormone imbalances, you should seek support from a hormone expert right now. If your body isn't functioning properly, then it's hard for you to be at your best, and I know how awesome you are, so talk to an expert, they just might have the answer

We could write a whole book on hormones, many people have, but that is neither my area of expertise nor is it the point of this book. But, I believe hormones play a part in our Boss Mom lives and just in case they affect you in a significant way, I wanted to address the topic.

I asked Celeste Coffman, a Licensed Professional Counselor and Certified School Counselor with over a decade of experience in the mental health and education industries, to provide a little insight into hormones and how they can affect us.

This is what she said . . .

"You're being so hormonal!" While it can be incredibly irritating to hear that statement, the majority of my female clients report mood swings, appetite changes, libido shifts and sleep woes that are all part of the hormonal fluctuations happening throughout the full month of their menstrual cycle and even during or after pregnancy or menopause.

Hormones, which are chemicals naturally found in the body, serve as regulators for virtually all bodily functions. Think of them as the Project Managers that stimulate cells into doing their specific jobs, whether it be maintaining body temperature, triggering sleep, or aiding in digestive processes.

Cortisol is the hormone produced in the adrenal system and released when we experience stress or fear. While cortisol gets a bad reputation, it's actually helpful in small doses. The release of cortisol is meant to aid our bodies in overcoming perceived threats to our safety. For example, if you're hiking in the woods and are confronted by a Grizzly, cortisol floods your body with the resources to fight harder and run faster.

Because most cells in the body have cortisol receptors, this powerful little hormone can affect virtually all bodily functions. Brain processes, reproduction, inflammation responses, blood sugar levels, metabolism, and many more are affected by the cortisol uptick we experience when confronted with threats (real or perceived). Since cortisol touches so many parts of the body, it's easy to see that weight gain, high blood pressure, and heart disease can easily be affected by too much cortisol in the bloodstream.

When explaining stress hormones, I like to compare them to sprinklers. As I write this, the sticky heat of southern summer is upon us, and a refreshing run through the sprinkler feels marvelous. A couple quick passes help us cool down and recharge. Imagine instead if I parked myself beside the sprinkler all day. At first, it's refreshing, but after a few hours, I would notice my fingers and toes wrinkling up. The constant slap-slap-slap of water would begin to sting my skin. The natural oils on my face would wash away, and my eyes would begin to sting after a while. If I stayed in the sprinkler non-stop for an entire day, my body temperature couldn't regulate appropriately when the sun goes down. I wouldn't be able to sleep with a constant spatter of water slapping me. What was once helpful for the moment has now become detrimental because of continuous exposure. It's the same with cortisol!

In addition to affecting our physical health, high levels of cortisol can have significant impact on your emotional health. Even anxiety and depression are linked to sky-high cortisol levels, and studies suggest that life expectancy is lowered as a result of consistently elevated cortisol. Still, many of us don't realize we are under continuous stress (or if we do, we try to power through).

Are you surprised that stress can come from both positive and negative situations? The Holmes-Rhae Life Stress Inventory is a list of 43 life events ranging from taking a vacation to losing a loved one. Users mark which of the 43 events they've experienced during the last year, and then their score indicates how likely the user is to experience "stress-induced health breakdown." Sounds frightening, right?

If you're curious to discover whether hormonal shifts might be affecting your mental and physical health, I ask you to commit to detailed monitoring of your moods and physical symptoms for at least 30 days (but preferably 60). While this sounds like an intense commitment, there are two simple ways to achieve the goal:

1. Print a monthly calendar (or use your day planner) and develop

symbols or colors that allow you to quickly chart things like your mood, your sleep, your appetite, and physical pain.

2. Download the app Period Tracker Lite, which allows you to simply click each day on any of the pre-listed 50+ moods or symptoms, or to customize your own. You also have plenty of room to type in notes, such as whether you had a crazy day at work for some particular reason or if you didn't sleep well due to sick kids.

After 30-60 days of tracking, you're likely to find some patterns. If simple behavior changes help comfort you during these hormonal shifts, that's wonderful. If not, consider using your tracking information to visit your doctor. I've found that it can be much easier to work with healthcare providers when armed with written details of your symptoms versus just trying to explain "feeling 'off' some days." Using monitoring charts or apps helps patients be taken more seriously during doctor visits.

Hormones, especially cortisol, are blamed for a world of problems (possibly disproportionately in women). However, these little Project Managers also regulate important functions in our bodies and deserve a little respect! Keeping your hormones well-balanced with good health care, sound nutrition, quality sleep, and regular stress management will keep your body and mind strong.

*Sources: http://www.hormone.org/hormones-and-health/what-do-hormones-do/cortisol

https://www.psychologytoday.com/blog/the-athletes-way/201301/cortisol-why-the-stress-hormone-is-public-enemy-no-1

https://www.stress.org/holmes-rahe-stress-inventory/

Menstruation

Did you know I plan my business around my period? Yep, I sure do. Why? You might ask. Well, because I run a better business when I acknowledge that I am a woman and that means there are certain times of the month when I am not at my best.

I remember I used to get upset when someone would tell me that a woman should not be a CEO because she would make irrational decisions while she was on her period . . . And yes, someone has said that to me before, and I don't think they were joking.

I disagree with them, but I do recognize that the hormone imbalances that happen during a woman's cycle can absolutely impact how we feel, act and react. These hormonal imbalances can be more or less drastic for each woman, but for me and those around me, it is noticeable.

This is usually how my month goes...

Five days before my period - I am a productive rock star. I get so much done that it feels like I could take over the world. It feels a bit like nesting when you are pregnant. This is an indicator that I am about to dip into a low soon. I try to schedule strategy, planning, and creation at this time.

Three days before my period - My brain still works as it should, but I don't feel like doing anything. I have this growing urge to bundle up with hot tea and binge watch my favorite show on Netflix. Trying to get work done at this point takes me twice as long, so I try to plan more interviews, editing as opposed to creating, and more down time.

During my period - I am more tired than usual, and I get frustrated more often. I make sure that my husband knows that I won't think his jokes are funny and I lose my patience with the kids quicker. However, because I am aware of my state of mind, I can proactively remove myself from situations that elicit a negative reaction. I make sure not to schedule team meetings or prospect calls during this time.

Immediately after my period – All of a sudden I notice I have more patience with my kids and husband, and I begin to appreciate his sense of humor again. I am back to normal. I really enjoy this time because I feel like a normal person that isn't thinking about my hormones or period. This time is all about getting some great work done and being with my family.

Ten days before my next period - Something funny happens that makes everyone happy. I am all about the sexy time. I am not ashamed to say it because I think we should all embrace these times and prepare for them. This is when date nights, putting the kids to bed early, or getting hubby to come home for a lunch date, are perfect. I am also back in the swing of being super productive and motivated.

For me, this cycle happens every month and is predictable. The only thing that throws everything off is if I am in a prolonged stressful situation like I was in the months leading up to my first Boss Mom Retreat. I started my period a whole week early, and it affected my entire business schedule. It took me months to get back on track so that my business tasks were set around my peak performance times. If you are going to plan your business around your menstruation cycle as I do, then make sure to include a little self-love in there because stress can throw a wrench in your business plans.

A friend once told me that she has never noticed a hormonal difference when she's on her period, and I have to admit that I was a bit jealous. Although I am so happy that this is not a challenge she has to deal with, for many of us this is a monthly cycle, and if you can learn to strategically plan around it, then you can use it to your advantage.

Pregnancy

Six weeks after I quit my job I took a 6-hour drive to Chicago to visit one of my best friends. I needed to get out of the house. It turned out that starting your own business was harder than I had originally imagined. We had all sorts of plans to party in the city, and we didn't want to waste any time. I jokingly mentioned that I was 'late' and hopefully I wasn't pregnant because that would cut into our plans to drink wine all night. My friend happened to work for a medical supply company and offered up a whole bottle of medical grade pregnancy tests just in case, you know the kind in doctors' offices. I took the test and was pink line free; we had the go-ahead to party like rock stars. We ate sushi, drank wine, danced, and had an amazing weekend.

I went home and days passed and still no period. I broke out the pregnancy tests and decided to give it another try. A few minutes in, a faint pink line started to appear. It was so faint I didn't know what to think, so I called my mom. She excitingly informed me that any line at all means that I am pregnant. Honestly, I didn't know how to feel. The first pang of guilt found its way into my mind as I wondered if partying that past weekend would end up having a negative effect on my pregnancy.

I must have had that pregnancy look of terror mixed with excitement on my face when my husband came home because it only took him one guess. We were going to have a baby. The next three months were spent learning the stages of the baby and figuring out what you are supposed to do when you are pregnant. I didn't have time to wonder what kind of mom I would be; I was too busy trying to get myself to believe I was really going to be a mom.

During most of my pregnancy I never felt guilty, I was mainly pissed off that I was tired and nauseous so much of the time. I wanted to work on my business and found it hard to concentrate and focus for the first four months. Once the morning sickness passed, I had a supercharge of energy and motivation. Of course, that is when the stress set in that there was a looming deadline when my new little one would come into the world. I never gave myself enough credit for the work I was doing, which was making a new human being. Those days when I was too exhausted to get more than two hours of work done, I was building lungs. Once I got my energy back my little baby was growing and my nausea transformed into that uncomfortable phase where you feel like you just ate five huge burritos, and your body is stretching. It was hard to think about anything else.

As I moved into the final trimester, my husband's jokes became less and less entertaining to me. Everything was uncomfortable and irritating. I started to wonder what life would be like as a new parent. I started to realize that I was now bound to my husband forever and that was a bit scary. I was lucky to find a man I loved, and we had enjoyed marriage for two years before we got pregnant, but having kids put that 'forever' thing to a new level. I can only imagine how many hormones were coursing through my body at that time because I was a crazy person most of the time, or at least I felt that way.

I had what the doctor called a "textbook pregnancy." She said it unfolded just the way it was supposed to. WHAT? Sure, I had a few fun times growing a baby, and sure I loved feeling my baby kick, but it was mostly pain, discomfort, irritation, and fear. THAT WAS TEXTBOOK? If you had a 'non-textbook' experience, then I send the biggest bear hug your way because growing a baby is hard. There were a lot of times that I made it look easy. I would put on a dress and get all dolled up and go out with my husband for a dinner and movie, but inside I was uncomfortable and scared.

I remember a close friend who was nine months pregnant threw a bachelorette party for a mutual friend. We had the party at my place in Chicago because I lived in the city at the time and then went out to a fun dance club in Wrigley. I didn't think much of it at the time, but after I had kids, I would think back to how uncomfortable she must have been that whole night and how she always had a smile on her face. She was and is still my hero.

I know that women are made to have children, and I am so grateful and honored that I have the ability to make life, but let's not sugar coat it, making life is hella hard. So if you feel like you shouldn't complain that you feel uncomfortable or remind your partner a million times that 'you' had the baby, don't you fret; you DID grow that baby from scratch, and that is worth something. My kids are two and four, and I still remind my husband that I was the one that actually grew those babies and brought them to life. My husband doesn't think it's that impressive these days, but I like to remind him from time to time anyway.

– Dana Malstaff

Postpartum

I was fortunate that I never dealt with postpartum mood disorder. I cried and had a some tough times, but overall I was once again 'textbook' when it came to post-pregnancy hormones. There are so many women out there who were not so lucky. Here is one story that stands out.

In 2012, I got pregnant unexpectedly. I was unprepared for how hard pregnancy would be on my body. I gave birth under a system called the "laborist model." This meant that the doctor who treated me throughout my pregnancy would not deliver my baby. Instead, the residents and attending on duty at the hospital would be in charge. I did not realize how much of an issue this would cause until I ended up in labor for 72 hours. I ended up having an emergency C-section and lost too much blood. The hospital delayed my blood transfusion by 36 hours and my recovery period was slow and painful. I was in and out of consciousness and was unable to feed my daughter right away.

On my three-month maternity leave from my corporate job, I cried a lot. Ordinarily, I am a vocal person, but during the first three months of my daughter's life, I hid my emotions. I never told my husband that I cried from the time he left until the time he came home. At the time, we lived in a third story apartment and had downsized to one car to save money. This was the first time in my life that I felt trapped.

Before getting pregnant, I was an extremely independent career-driven woman. I came and went as I pleased, and I always made enough money to support myself. Many times, postpartum depression is categorized by the mother not bonding with her child, but this was not the case for me. I had no problem bonding with my daughter. Since I didn't have a hard time connecting with her, I did not understand that something was going on that needed to be treated.

When I returned to my corporate job in early 2013, I got promoted and started traveling more for work. At the time, this was my escape from dealing with my postpartum depression. I quickly realized that being a working mom in corporate America was extremely difficult. I decided that if no one else was going to talk about the harsh realities of being a new mom in corporate America, then I would. This was when I decided to start my blog, Redefining Mom. Initially, my blog was just a place to vent and share the story of my difficult transition back to corporate. It became therapeutic to share my story with other people, and I quickly realized that my story resonated with a lot of other moms.

Blogging helped me cope with my feelings of distress and sadness that life seemed much harder for me than other working moms. I saw so many other women at work that appeared to have it all figured out and I was struggling to keep it together. Finally, at the urging of a new OB/GYN doctor, I started seeing a postpartum therapist that diagnosed me with Postpartum PTSD due to birth trauma. The diagnosis provided clarity to me in an otherwise dark cloud of confusion and isolation. **Simply understanding that what I was going through was real, and there was an explanation for why everything seemed so difficult, gave me an immense amount of hope.** It was because of this diagnosis and the therapy that followed that I was able to accept that my dream of a corporate career was no longer what I wanted.

Little did I know at the time, but launching my blog would provide the confidence I needed to pull the plug on my corporate career. Blogging provided an outlet to share my story with other moms. Once I was diagnosed with Postpartum PTSD, and I shared it with my audience, I received countless emails from women telling me that my story inspired and gave them the courage to seek help for themselves.

Before the birth of my daughter, I thought that, deep down, I wanted to be a stay-at-home mom. Since maternity leave turned out to be possibly the toughest three months of my life, I emphatically believed that I was meant to be a corporate working mom and chase the career goals that I had spent so long working towards. Neither proved to be true, and the most valuable lesson was learning to accept that I play many different roles in my life. I am a mom, wife, daughter, sister, friend, and I am still me. I still have thoughts, feelings, dreams, and goals that have nothing to do with being a mom. So often, women are 'guilted' into feeling as if self-sacrificing your hopes and dreams for your kids is the only way to be a good mom. **I emphatically believe that I am the best version of myself and I am the best mother I can be when I allow myself the opportunity to do things that feed my creativity and ambition.**

It took me three years to finally accept that I no longer wanted to work in corporate. In 2015, I was invited to the White House to share my experience as a working mom in the United States, and it changed my life. I decided that if the White House cared enough to listen to what I had to say then I could use my experiences to help other women. I quit my corporate career in August 2016. I now run an online business that helps working moms transition out of corporate by building their own online businesses.

When the road seems too dark to travel, remember that there is light on the other side. Living with Postpartum PTSD for almost two years made life seem like a very long dark road with nothing waiting for me at the other end. The best advice I can give someone who is traveling this same road is to ask for help. No matter how difficult it seems, this too shall pass. There are wonderful communities you can find through Facebook groups for all sorts of topics like postpartum problems, supportive working moms, and empowering mom entrepreneurs. Remember, you are not alone!

– Monica Froese

Menopause

Before I turned 40, I started getting hot flashes, and my body started changing. I was gaining weight even though nothing in my day-to-day actions had changed. I went to my doctor for an annual check-up, and she wanted to do blood work because she thought my thyroid was the culprit. I thought it was menopause, but she said I was younger than usual and that it was most likely something else. I had this gut feeling, but everyone kept telling me I was wrong.

Right around this same time, I decided to start my own business. I had been a six-figure earner in the workplace, and I wanted to make that same income with my own business.

Because of the weight gain, hot flashes, and hormone imbalance I had major insecurities and the new business caused doubt and fear on an almost constant basis.

When she could not find a reason for my symptoms, my doctor finally ordered the right tests and confirmed that I WAS going through menopause. I had known it all along, but now everyone else believed it too. That time in my life was very difficult because I was not sure how to handle my elevated emotions and I often felt like my business building was going way too slow. It took a while, but I was able to get my hormones normalized, and I began to see more momentum and movement in my business.

Through this time in my life, I have realized the importance of self-care. I am not talking about the get a manicure self-care, I am talking about giving myself space and really listening to my body. I have to make sure that I don't get consumed by my business or overpromise. I have to listen when my body tells me it needs a break and give myself grace when my hormones affect my emotions and how I interact with those I love.

If you are going through menopause, then my heart goes out to you lady, because it can be tough and it can last for years. Your body will change in strange ways, and sometimes you will instantaneously get irritated and hot. This is all normal, and while it might drive you crazy, there are things you can do to manage this challenging time in your life.

First, don't ignore this change in your life. You will need to give yourself time to get to know how your body reacts to this new environment and then adjust how you approach your business and relationships accordingly. And second, know that it will get better and that there will be light at the end of the tunnel. I am still in the thick of it, and some days drive me crazy, but there are also wonderful days in between where I am productive and blissful. In these times in our lives when it all seems too tough to bear, remember that you are not alone, and what you are feeling is normal. Get the support you need to get through it and remember that we are here to wave the fan on your face when those hot flashes hit.

– Natalie Gingrich

* * * *

Sometimes life feels like a perfect storm. Sometimes we get pissed off because someone said something that hit us right in the heart. Sometimes you are just tired from working late the night before, and your kid has a nightmare, and you don't get any sleep.

Sometimes hormones have nothing to do with it; we are just having a bad day.

You are allowed to get angry, upset, frustrated, or sad for no real reason. We are allowed to act crazy sometimes, and I think we should stop beating ourselves up so much because the fact is that every person on earth has bad days and that's ok.

I believe that the more we become conscious of how our bodies work, the easier it is to sense when something is wrong and do something about it. That might be as small as removing ourselves from a situation so we have time to breath before we react, or it might feel like a larger persisting issue where we need to see a doctor so you can try to understand what's going on.

Either way, we need to stop denying the fact that as women we function differently than men and that it's nothing to be ashamed of, in fact, we should embrace being a woman and all that comes with it.

We should be more open with the world about how we feel and what is affecting us. We should seek help sooner for emotions we don't feel like we can control.

We should try to understand our unique bodies and how they react so that we can quickly identify when something is wrong.

And we should find other women who understand how we feel so that we aren't surrounded by people who make us feel bad for who we are and negate our challenges.

HARDSHIP & LOSS

Life isn't always fair, in fact, sometimes it is downright cruel. Since the inception of Boss Mom, I have heard hundreds of stories from amazing women who have been dealt hardships that fill my heart with empathy and sadness. Some of these stories are profoundly sad and might make you cry; I know that in writing this book I have shed many tears, and I think that's a good thing.

Even though these stories involve serious loss and emotional trials, they are also about finding a new path and moving forward. While none of the following stories are mine, I feel connected to their stories and their challenges. Each one of these women wanted to regain control of their lives, and many of them became Boss Moms to find themselves again, connect with a community, and move forward.

Get your tissues ready and know that if you resonate with one of these stories, the Boss Mom community is here to support and love you. Know that you are not alone, not now, and not in the future, so make sure you reach out so that we can embrace you with all the love and compassion we have to give.

Low Self-Image

Let me take you back to a moment in time. It was during summer break, and my son was two at the time. My husband, my son, and I took a weekend trip out to my parent's cabin. The weather was beautiful, the sun was shining, and life was good—or so I thought. My son and husband were walking together holding hands a few feet in front of me on the dirt road. I reached my hand into my pocket for my phone and snapped a lovely photograph of the two of them. A Kodak moment of sorts.

When we returned home, I began to scroll through my photographs on my phone. Aw, there was the precious picture I had taken of the two of them walking hand-in-hand. Then I came across another picture my son's first pet, again a picture of my husband and son. My son's first bath in the sink, his first time at the zoo, once again all pictures of my husband and son. **It was at that moment looking through the photographs that I began to cry, as the more pictures I scrolled through, I realized I wasn't in any of them.** It was because I was ashamed of my body and my weight, I stood behind the camera instead of in front of it, and for the first two years of my son's life, there is no pictorial record of his mother being present and sharing in those milestone moments.

I was ashamed, dejected, crushed, and pissed off. **My two-year-old son didn't care what size, or shape his momma was, but for some reason I did, and it cost me moments and memories.**

Now I want to tell you that my life-defining moment was not because I had a serious illness. I didn't survive a car crash or suffer trauma as a child. I simply was a mom who was stuck in a rut. And, because I was sick and tired of being sick and tired and missing out on the milestones, I decided one day to change my life for the better. I took it one day at a time, one step at a time. There was nothing miraculous that happened overnight, and my life didn't become magically better. It started with the decision to take action, and, with perseverance, it improved over time.

And if you're a mom who has ever thought, "please don't take a picture of me because my hair isn't done," or because your butt might look slightly big in those pants, or you don't have makeup on. I tell you to throw caution to the wind and jump in! Be the mom who has her hair in a 2-day pony making silly faces in the pictures. Be the mom who is celebrating every milestone right next to her child. Because while I was hiding behind the camera lens, I was hiding from myself, hiding from my life, and hiding from my potential.

Deep down I knew that hiding wasn't the answer. I had to go deep within myself and ask if I was willing to miss being an active part of my son's memories because I was worried that my body wasn't good enough. When I answered that question truthfully, I began to realize that I was stuck in a rut! And you know what it all boils down to? Worthiness. Because if I truly believe that I was worthy of living an amazing life, I would be. On some level, being stuck and staying in that rut meant that I didn't feel worthy of the life I desired

I decided that to get myself out of the rut was to put myself on my own calendar. You know, the big mama calendar that we all have on our fridge. The one that you walk up to every day and it is littered with everybody else's activities, except for yours. And my name was nowhere to be found on that thing. I put myself on the calendar amongst the gymnastics, soccer, and hockey abyss, and I made that time non-negotiable!

We all know that life is busy, as moms we are busy, we wear it like a badge of honor, but let's not die on the BUSY cross. We have to-do lists that are miles long—laundry, lunches, cleaning toilets, buying groceries, making meals, drive to dancing, load the dishwasher. And where was I on that to-do list? NOWHERE! Because as mamas we take care of and nurture everyone else and their needs, and tend to ourselves last.

My advice is to drop the mama guilt because it's not serving anyone. **Show your children that their mother is worth the time taken to spend on herself.** Would you ever say to your child, "Go to school, but no daydreaming about what you want to be when you grow up (because no one has time for that) and be sure to stifle those dreams and desires. Love you! Have a great day!" NO! So why do you think it's okay to tell yourself that every day?

These days, when I pull out my camera I'm no longer hiding behind it, we are all in for a full-on groupie selfie, where smiles, tickles, snorts, giggles, laughs, and love abounds.

– Laurie Joy

You Can't Afford to be a SAHM

I returned to work after my maternity leave in February of 2016. I dreaded that day with every ounce of my being. I loved being home with my daughter all day. It was challenging and tiring, yet the most meaningful job in the world for me. I wanted that immense responsibility of shaping her life, manners, experiences, schedule, and character day in and day out. Further, my career as a school counselor was stressful.

I loved parts of it, but I was emotionally drained at the end of the day after handling one crisis after another. I was wiped out when I got home, and with my husband and I both working all day, the evening was rushing to put a healthy, homemade dinner on the table, pack homemade pureed food and pumped bottles of breastmilk for daycare, pack lunches for my husband and me, then get my daughter fed, bathed, and to bed. My time with her became so limited. I wanted more than an hour in the morning and two hours in the evening.

This was not the mom life I wanted. I knew I wanted to be a stay-at-home mom before we had kids, but financially, our family could not pay the bills on my husband's income. Pre-baby, this was a reality I accepted and assumed I'd just get used to. It was normal. I worked with lots of teachers who longed to be at home with their kids, but they still got through each day. I figured that was my destiny too.

My husband and I had many conversations about my desire to stay home. The conversations always ended with how we couldn't afford it. I was bringing home half our income each month PLUS providing our family's awesome health insurance. I felt utterly stuck. But this was a pill I just couldn't force myself to swallow. I didn't want to settle. If I'm totally raw, deep inside, I wanted my husband to say he'd take on extra work to make up the income we needed. I never thought I wanted to be "taken care of" by my husband. After all, I was the first in my family to get my master's degree then paid off $50,000 in student loan debt in 2.5 years on two meager starting teacher salaries. I was driven and had an "I can take care of myself" attitude.

My mom was a working mom, but I have two older sisters who both stay-at-home. I've seen the amazing job they've done raising independent, respectful, confident, and healthy children. I longed to have the same opportunity. I was jealous their husbands were entrepreneurs and worked their rear ends off to sustain their family financially. However, I also saw the sacrifice that brought. Their massive working hours left my sisters acting as single moms many days. That wasn't what I wanted either, and my husband didn't offer to take on that role.

So, what could I do? We needed more income, and I wasn't happy in my job. I missed my daughter. I could not accept this as our life for the next five years. I would deeply regret it. I toyed with the idea of in-home daycare or bartending evenings and weekends. Neither sounded appealing, but it was a start.

When I talked to one sister about wanting to stay home, she mentioned her husband was working a second full-time job creating an online business. He was earning a legitimate income, and the future was even brighter. She asked him to Skype with me about options for earning money from home. I was hooked. This was it. I had no clue what I was doing, but I was determined to make it work. He was a mentor to me, and for his knowledge and time, I am forever grateful. He knew my financial goal and made me believe I could achieve it without returning to work the next school year. I wasn't sure, but I knew I'd give it my all.

I woke up at 4:30 a.m. most days and stayed up late researching and learning as much as I could. The drive to be a work-from-home mom was intense. I also turned to my faith. I prayed intensely, and God delivered.

Four months after my return from maternity leave, the school year ended and my contract for the next year came. It had a hefty raise. I was looking at an offer $3,000 more than I'd earned the year before, and $13,000 higher than my first contract four years ago. I had doubts. How could I walk away from this predictable income? How could I put my family at risk for my own desires? Was I selfish? Was I crazy? Again, I prayed and hustled. My husband and I set a goal that by the end of the 2016-2017 school year, I'd earn $1,000 per month working from home. We had savings to get us through a year, but not more. After that, I'd either earn enough from home or return to work. I was nervous financially but jacked emotionally. I left that enticing contract unsigned, and instead signed a letter of resignation.

All summer, I locked myself away with my laptop starting my freelance editing and writing business whenever my husband was home with our daughter. I can't fathom the number of hours I put in without a penny of pay, but hard work pays off. It's now seven months after I learned what a website domain was, and I am earning $1,000 per month. . . even more some months.

I've learned I'm capable of so much more than I'd imagined. I work more hours now, but it's more meaningful work. I get to see the impact I'm making on my daughter every day. And I discovered I love writing and editing. We didn't dip into our emergency fund at all, and we are expecting our second child this summer. I'm nervous about how to put in these working hours with a newborn and two-year-old, but I have every right to be confident in my abilities as an entrepreneur and mom. This is a life I never imagined for myself, but I am happy, proud, and blessed to be a Boss Mom.

My number one piece of advice for anyone else struggling with going back to work after having a little one is: Don't settle. Ask questions and research online. With enough motivation and determination, you can create the life you want. You don't have to settle for the "normal" path if that's not what you want. Create the path that will make you and your family happy, have faith, and dig in!

– Val Breit

You Get Sick

It was six years ago, I was 44-years-old and doing my best to keep up with the fast pace, over stressed, over worked life I had created for myself. I had three kids, a daughter who was thirteen and two sons who were seven and nine. I ran a full-time research business from home, played tennis, worked out regularly with a trainer and managed to run a household that very rarely skipped a beat. I was married to my best friend from college, but we had forgotten how to make each other a priority.

I wasn't feeling well, and my doctor insisted it was a virus but I knew deep down it was something more. He suggested I go home and rest and take some vertigo medicine to help with the dizziness. I was always good at listening to my gut and this time turned out to be no exception. I insisted on having a colonoscopy that my regular doctor said could wait another six years. As I sat across the desk from my GI doctor with a can of ginger ale in my hand I heard him mumble something. I don't recall much of the conversation since I was still groggy from the sedative but what I heard was blah, blah, blah, blah, cancer.

I knew from this point on my life would be forever changed. I was scared and unsure of my future, but I knew I was exactly where I was supposed to be, and somehow everything was going to work out for the best.

The hardest part about my diagnosis was that I began living

my life from a place of fear instead of a place of love. My children were young, and my first instinct was to protect them. I didn't want them to go through life without a mom. I became fanatical about all things that could cause cancer and as a result scared my children half to death. I cut out all animal protein and dairy and removed all sugar and processed foods from our pantry. I would glare at my kids when we were out and ordered bacon or other cold cuts with nitrates that might cause cancer. I was spreading fear throughout our home and not explaining my reasons for why we as a family should be eating and living a healthier lifestyle. I was learning the science behind what to eat, but I was not communicating that to my family in a way that would help us all grow and evolve.

Instead of living and enjoying each day with my family, I was focused on what I could tightly control to ensure that the cancer never returned. I had to relearn how to communicate in a way that allows me to express my feelings and learn to just slow down, breathe and sit quietly with myself. But the biggest takeaway for me has been the concept of trusting that my challenges are not here to knock me down but rather to help me see the hidden gifts and beauty that have been available to me all along.

Synchronicity keeps me going. The simple act of becoming aware of coincidental events and finding the meaning in them is extremely powerful. The night before my very first surgery I was staring out my bedroom window and saw a beautiful butterfly land on the light post. It just sat there for a long time occasionally flapping its wings but not moving much. I knew in my heart at this moment that everything was going to be OK. I was ready for the transformation that was ahead of me and knew it would be tough and take work, but I also knew that I was exactly where I was supposed to be and that something beautiful would soon emerge. Today, my kids and I see lots of butterflies. They hang out with us when we are lounging in tubes in the pool, land on my side view mirror when stopped at a light in the car, and sit quietly on the rose bushes when we are throwing a ball for our dog to chase.

My family and friends are what keep me motivated to stay well. Before each surgery I would think positive thoughts about all the fun things still left to do with my children. When I look back, I know that this path was here for me so I could learn to make needed changes. I have a type A personality and needed to be hit over the head really hard before I would hear any of the subtle messages that were encouraging me to slow down and take care of myself. **I learned that life is about so much more than all that we can accomplish in a single day.**

I threw away the badge of honor I wore for getting the most done in the shortest amount of time while having three small children. I learned that my husband would drop everything for me when I needed him the most—while sleeping in a hospital chair is not fun, he never complained. I learned that I was a poor communicator and had to work on better ways to express how I feel. I learned that eating the right foods is an incredibly important step towards healing from illness, but it is only one piece of a much larger puzzle.

For anyone dealing with illness, remember to come at life from a place of love. Fear keeps us stuck in the past and longing for the future. Concentrate on living in the present, and you will begin to see your very own synchronicities unfolding right in front of your eyes. Be patient, if your journey is bumpy, there are plenty of reasons for your struggles, and sometimes the messages are not revealed to you until much later in life. Embrace who you are—each and every imperfect piece of you and always make time for your children, no matter how old they have become!

– Marietta Goldman

* * * *

Everyone has his or her own path in discovering what they want to be when they grow up. Mine, well, it was unconventional, to say the least. Becoming a photographer wasn't in my life plans. I wasn't inspired by famous names or drawn in by the thought of starting my own business. Instead, photography found me. When I had my daughter in 2004, I asked my husband to buy us a DSLR camera so we can take pictures of her. How hard could it be to figure out, right? I was wrong. It was very hard. So after briefly trying out the camera, and not "getting it" right away, I got frustrated. Instead, put the camera away and allowed it to gather dust for quite some time. I was a stay-at-home mom at the time, and loving it!

My daughter and I took music classes together, went on play dates and spent every minute enjoying each other while she was growing. Before I knew it, she was off to preschool, and it was the perfect time to have another baby. I was very lucky with my daughter. I got pregnant very easily. I assumed the same would happen the second time around. I was right. Just a few months into trying I was once again pregnant. My 8-week appointment went beautifully. We saw a little heartbeat, and everything looked great. I was giddy with excitement. It was so hard to keep it a secret. I was already showing. Even if I didn't tell anyone, they knew! I lay in bed at night dreaming about my perfect little family that was soon to be.

A few weeks later, my gut told me something wasn't right. Sadly, my instincts were correct. On Christmas Eve, at my 12-week appointment, the doctor broke the new to us. The baby stopped growing at ten weeks. There was no heartbeat. My husband and I decided to try again a few months later. Again, a few months in, I got pregnant! I was overrun with joy once again. I was hoping this time would be it and that it would help ease the pain of the miscarriage. A week after my positive pregnancy test, I was on the way to Florida for a planned family vacation. That morning I felt small cramps in my abdomen. By the time the plane landed, I was doubled over in pain. I went straight to the ER. The doctors told me I was having another miscarriage. They gave me some pain pills and told me to "hang in there."

The pain, both physical and emotional, was unbearable. Upon my second visit to the ER (after the pain medication wouldn't work) I was told again just to wait for my body to take care of what it needed to. Well, I waited. And waited. The waiting was torture. I was stuck in bed, and all I could think is how I couldn't believe this was happening again. What was wrong with me? Why couldn't I keep a baby? What did I do to deserve this?

We returned to New York and saw my OB/GYN. She was confused. She performed a sonogram but couldn't see anything. She sent me to a local radiology office for some further testing. The tech in the radiology office quickly told me to get dressed and wait in the waiting area. A few minutes later, the nurse put me on the phone with my doctor. I can hear the words in her voice in my head so clearly even today. She said "**Mrs. Rozenbaum, I want you to ask the receptionist for your records. If she can't produce them in the next minute, just leave and meet me at the hospital. You** had an ectopic pregnancy that ruptured. You have been internally bleeding for four days, and if you don't have surgery in the next hour or so, you will die."

Die.

Do you know what it's like when someone tells you that you are going to die? I was like stone. Numb. I rushed to the emergency room, and they immediately admitted me. The funny thing is I remember the doctor telling me that I was, most likely, going to lose my ovaries. That is when I finally felt something. I felt a gaping hole in my stomach. A pit that would make the Grand Canyon seem like a pothole. Rolling into the OR, I remember thinking this could be it. Was I going to die? Was it possible I couldn't have any more children? The gravity of either possibility was equally as heavy. I ended up losing a fallopian tube. The doctor was able to save my ovaries. Everyone told me how lucky I was that I was alive.

For the first time in a long time, however, I didn't feel so lucky. It's not that I wanted to die, but being alive was painful. I felt depressed. **I felt I couldn't protect my children—even inside me.** I felt like a failure, less of a woman. I was anxious. Angry. Sad. Confused. I didn't know if there was any hope of me having another baby. I didn't know what to say to all the people that told me "it was time to have another." I didn't know how to tell my daughter she might not ever have any siblings. I didn't know how to tell my husband I may not be able to give him the family he wanted.

When my daughter was at school, I was bored and alone with my thoughts. The thoughts were plaguing me. It's because of this I knew I had to find a distraction. I needed an escape from my sadness, frustration and the constant questions in my mind as to why this happened. It was then that my husband reminded me of the camera gathering dust in the closet. I pulled it out, dusted it off, and gave it a whirl. I didn't know it at the time, but that was the start of my photography journey and my work with women. **My camera saved me.** It was my friend and confidant when I needed it most. It helped me see beauty in the world again. It opened my eyes to incredible women that struggled with their femininity for varied reasons. They were just like me! It was therapy.

As I started talking about my fertility issues, I started hearing more stories from other women about theirs. They whisper when they tell me. They feel shame. I felt shame. I got it. I don't know why, though? Why do we feel shame over something we cannot control?

I was very blessed to welcome a son into my family in 2009; I was able to have another child after all.

I love my children more than I can ever explain. But it doesn't mean that I have forgotten the ones I didn't have. The difference now is that I can speak about it, shamelessly.

Letting go of the shame hasn't always come easily. Sadly, women are shamed every day. We are shamed for things such as working, staying home, being too thin or fat. The list goes on and on. We feel our own shame deep down. We allow others to shame us as well. My life's work as an intimate photographer for women is dedicated to helping women celebrate their unique femininity, shamelessly. It never ceases to amaze me how the universe works its magic. A terrible time in my life quickly led to a flourishing business and connections with many shameless women. The women I have photographed all tell me how I have impacted their lives. The truth is they have impacted mine tenfold. They have inspired me and made me brave. They have humbled me. Most importantly, they have healed me.

From all of this, I learned that life is always full of curve balls. Patience is a virtue because even though you may not understand why something is happening at the moment, it will make sense looking back. I carry this into my life now, whenever I am going through a hard time I remember it will be ok, even if I am not sure when that will be.

All of the great success stories in this world came out of hard times. Embrace the hard times, as I always say "Run towards the pain." On the other side of pain, there is always something amazing waiting.

−Jen Rosenbaum

Someone You Love Gets Sick

2014 was a year of joy, turmoil, and change. Lots and lots of change. It all began in March, just nine months after leaving my full-time job and becoming a full-time entrepreneur. I was giving birth to my son and half way through pushing, a code was called, additional doctors, nurses, and the anesthesiologist were called into the room. My son was born blue, limp, and unresponsive. While I was lucky and they were able to resuscitate him, the trials didn't end there. My son refused to eat for six hours after birth and lost one pound before leaving the hospital, which is a lot of weight to lose for a newborn baby. He began to recover, and we were released from the hospital to start our lives as parents.

A few weeks later my husband woke up in pain. He was sent to the hospital for CT scans which later showed he had appendicitis and would need surgery. I wish the turmoil ended here, but this was just the beginning of the scariest time of my life. The CT scan also showed a growth on his kidney. One that had been there for three years. We saw specialists and were told it was a 50% chance that it was cancer. We scheduled the surgery for the end of June when my husband would have enough time to take off of work. In May, we prepped our condo and began the listing process. In June, we began showing it and received an offer close to my husband's surgery. His surgery went well; we went to stay with my mom where I would have extra help with the kids and my husband as he healed.

Ten days later was the start of one of the worst weeks of my life. My husband was suddenly in excruciating pain, and my mom rushed him to the hospital as I put the kids to bed. As my mom was walking him into the hospital, he passed out and cracked his head on the parking lot curb. When I finally got to the hospital, he was in extreme pain and was being administered morphine every 15 minutes. They ran multiple CT scans and were scrambling to manage his pain and figure out what was happening. He was admitted to ICU and stayed there for another six days. He was bleeding out internally. While packing up our condo, I received a text from my husband that they were giving him a blood transfusion. I broke down. I was emotionally and physically exhausted, but I needed to be at my husband's side. He spent a few more days in the ICU after that and then another day in a regular bed for observation.

The day he was released from the hospital was the same day the movers came to get the furniture and take it to my mom's house. We hadn't found a home yet, so in the interim, we stayed with my mom. In October 2014 we finally found a home and things began to settle.

During this entire period, I had a business to run. I had clients to attend to. I wasn't just a mom and a wife. I was a business owner. It was this turmoil, this season of change, that began the biggest change in my business. You see, I didn't have any plans in place for maternity leave, let alone anything that would allow me to take the time I needed during this family emergency. I had clients emailing me and asking when their projects would be done while I was still in the hospital (after giving birth) and even when I was sitting in the ICU waiting room.

When I returned to work full-time, I had lost the passion, the drive. I didn't want to do it anymore. I started to question whether I was doing the right thing. I started searching for answers. After a year of pivots, tweaks, and changes, I realized it wasn't one thing that I needed to change, but several tweaks that needed to be made and a lot of planning.

The next year or so, showed me that it wasn't just what I was doing but who I was working with and the systems I had in place that needed to change. I needed to work with people that were the right fit for me. So I made the tweaks, I defined my dream clients, and I set out to find them. I signed up for coaching, made plans and put systems in place.

I now have a team, systems, amazing clients who are like friends, and a business I love. I work from home with my 3-year-old, which can sometimes be trying, but having these systems and plans in place makes everything run so much smoother. It's not fun thinking about worst case scenarios, but it's so important for you, your family and your business. If you're going through a season of turmoil or change, know that things will be ok and that you've got this. If you're just starting out or if you've been in business for a while, be sure that you set yourself up for success. Make plans, have systems and, best of all, have a support system, whether that's a team or just a group of awesome Boss Moms that know you, love you and encourage you.

– Samantha Johnston

Surviving Loss

Although I didn't know it at the time, my business would be born from the death of my infant daughter. To be honest, when times are difficult, when I don't feel like pushing forward anymore, I reflect on the reasons that I started doing what I do in the first place, I remember my WHY, and I push forward.

Infant and pregnancy loss is something that will shake any mother to the core, no matter how strong. If you've gone through this recently, I know you feel alone. I know you want to give everything up. I know you are questioning everything about your life and how you got there.

This is normal, Mama. I encourage you to not make any major life-altering decisions in the early days and months of grief. Because if this is where you find yourself now, you are probably, like I was at the time, incapable of seeing past the present moment. Forget about strategic plans and long-term goals; your goal right now is to get out of bed, to breathe, and to make it minute by minute.

I had only stopped working in my full-time job as a Homeland Security/Counter-Terrorism Planner about a month when I was blessed with my 3rd pregnancy. I was transitioning from full-time out of the home working mom to a stay-at-home mom of a 4-year-old and a 1-year-old. About five weeks into this not-so-easy transition, I learned I was pregnant. But not just with one baby.

There were two buns in the oven. I'll spare you the specific details, but briefly, the babies developed a syndrome that affects identical twins, Twin-to-Twin Transfusion Syndrome (TTTS), they were very sick, born at 30 weeks, and my baby Kathryn passed away at two days old from complications of TTTS.

How this led to my business? I started blogging as an outlet for my grief and to bring awareness to TTTS. That led to a book. I had no income, so I completed the entire process of self-publishing with little outside support. I learned the system and found that I loved it. That led to more books, to helping others with their books, and to my publishing house, Kat Biggie Press; named after my baby girl, Kathryn Bigwarfe.

I don't know how it would have affected my business if I had already been an entrepreneur when I lost her, but I do know that the grieving time is essential. You have to put everything else on hold to make it through. If it's not possible to put your entire business on hold, outsource what you can, prioritize everything, and only do the things that bring you joy. Share with your clients so that they understand why you may be absent. Automate everything you can to give yourself some breathing room.

Then feel all the feels. Don't try to suppress the grief and move on too quickly. I assure you, it will rear its ugly head later on if you don't allow yourself the time. Do things that make you happy and honor the baby. I threw myself into advocacy work and giving back to other grieving mothers, and then eventually into my business.

It doesn't seem possible in the worst of the grieving period, but there will be sunshine after the storm. It is okay to find happiness again one day and to press forward with "normal" life. You will eventually smile genuinely again. You will get through this. But don't be afraid to press the pause button on life and your business (if that's possible!) to get through the today.

— Alexa Bigwarfe

Haven't Been Able to Have Kids

In October 2016, I could just feel it, feel the differences I felt twice before but that have never worked out. You know, those changes you notice when you have been pregnant before and just know in the depths of your heart that "this will be our time." You wait, take the test, and there are those two lines you have been praying for, while faint, they're still there. You call the doctor; go in for confirmation, only to find out all of the three tests you took were false positives.

After two miscarriages and a false positive, our confidence in everything was shattered. Have you ever felt this way? Well, I have because this is my story. I am a small business and confidence coach who has lost her confidence in thinking I will be able to have children. It has been a roller coaster ride, at times I wish I could get off, but at the same time, I know that this is my journey.

Yup that is right, in the year and few months that my husband and I have been trying I have zero children but three angel babies and a false positive. Yet, in that year, while not being too silent about our struggles, I have been able to grow my business.

The difficult thing about not having kids but desperately wanting them is I feel like an imposter most of the time and it really eats away at me some days. It's not like I am a crazy "I want all the babies and get jealous over others kids," it's quite the opposite. I am so thrilled for others who are expecting or have children, but it is hard to not get down on myself for not being able to create life. Some days it's only a slight twinge of self-guilt and other days it's like "COME ON OVARIES AND UTERUS WORK ALREADY!" all while smiling and growing the business I love too, hence the imposter part.

At times it has been hard to talk about it with other moms or women who haven't had children yet. The worst things I hear Is "Oh don't worry your time will come." While I know it is said in good nature, at the time it cuts deep because I feel like maybe my time has passed. I have been married for almost five years, and my husband was the one who, about a year after getting married, said, "let's make a baby," (yes said to the tone of "Let's make a deal"). I was the one who kept him at arm's length for the better part of three years, always making excuses because I was scared and not ready. I felt like I needed to be at a certain level in my career or be making enough money to be "ready for kids."

I knew I wanted to be a mom one day, but it's as if my subconscious knew this would be a battle I could not do on my own. So in July of 2015, after my husband got back from his last deployment, and made the decision to leave the military, I finally said, "ok, I am on board for this." Which even as I am typing this seems so selfish, how dare I wait, how dare I want my husband to be here for the pregnancy. Obviously not only is the guilt of making my poor husband wait, but also putting him through the pain of knowing we CAN get pregnant, my body just isn't able to keep it. When you put that pressure on yourself, some days it can be deafening and defeating all at once; however, it is not all bad.

I've learned that while you may think you're ready and have a plan that the plan almost certainly never works out the way you want.

Even on the business side, the only constant is change. Embracing change, especially once I was diagnosed with Hoshimoto's Autoimmune Disorder—which is part of the struggle to carrying a baby to term—I could either fight it, or I could face it. I chose to face my struggles head on.

If you are in a similar situation where your business is thriving, but the mom life just hasn't happened for you yet, do not lose hope or faith, you will make it through this tough time. Have faith, keep pursuing and never doubt yourself.

– Nicole Hoglund

Separation and Divorce

I was at the start of year two of my business when my husband and I separated. For me, this was a critical time. The business was finally starting to grow, I was getting closer to my monthly income goals, and I had a steady client load. But suddenly, the business that I was building as a passion project and for supplemental income while safely supported by my husband's income, needed to pay for all of my bills and expenses. The stress of that alone caused me to make some bad business decisions. I panicked and took on too many clients or clients that I knew were not a good fit, just to ensure I would be able to make ends meet.

While I could pay the bills, the emotional wear and tear of the situation often made it difficult to focus. During this timeframe, I learned some valuable lessons. Early on in my business, I was told to keep my personal life separate from my business life. My clients didn't need to know what was going on behind the scenes.

But I'm going to tell you something different. When you're

69

traversing a major life situation, I believe you owe it to your clients to give them at least a head's up. You're not immune to having bad days under this type of stress. After breaking down during a client phone call and crying like a baby over mistakes I made on her project, I admitted to her that my personal life was in shambles. At first, I felt incredibly weak for sharing this. But afterward, I realized most people are compassionate, and she needed to know there was a legitimate reason for my missteps; that this was not an indication of my typical performance. Once I opened up to her, our relationship changed. I felt relieved that I would receive a second chance from her and she was pleased to know I trusted her enough to share the details.

If you are dealing with a separation or divorce, my heart goes out to you. It's a very difficult time in general, but especially for moms who run a business. Some days may feel like you're never going to make it. You will, but you're going to have to put on your big girl pants.

Some of the questions you should ask yourself include:

- Whether or not to share personal details with your clients?

- Should you be scaling back or pushing to grow?

- What will you need to be able to support yourself?

- How do you increase your revenue if you're not quite at a point to support yourself?

- Who is in your network that can be helpful to you during this time?

Now more than ever, it's important to dust off (or create) that strategic plan, understand your financial situation and resources, and fully examine all of your expenses and income so that you're able to pay yourself the amount you need to make ends meet.

There are many days when I wonder if I'll make it, or if I'll have to resort back to the good ole 9-5 to be able to pay the bills. But I keep pressing forward, I use my resources and my networks to get referrals, and I trust in the business that I built. You're going to be distracted and emotional during this time, so be kind to yourself. You can do amazing things.

– Alexa Bigwarfe

* * * *

These are only a fraction of the true stories of amazing women who are trying to make life work and pursue happiness. My fondest hope is that one of these stories spoke to you and can help you feel a little less alone.

What happens when you feel like you have had it pretty good? You have had your struggles for sure, but overall you are pretty happy, and you feel like you haven't had any significant struggles that other women talk about. You and your family are healthy, your husband is supportive, money isn't a major concern, and for the most part, life is pretty good. So you don't get to complain, right?

Wrong!

Your struggles and challenges don't have to be big to be impactful for you and those around you. Most of your life might be going fine, but that little thing that keeps nagging at you, or that sadness you feel every so often, is worthy of sharing, and you are allowed to feel that way.

Just because others might have experienced larger challenges than you, does not negate your right to acknowledge and voice your own struggles.

Let me be clear, I am not an advocate of being a constant complainer because I don't think it serves us in any positive way, but acknowledging your challenges is important. Once you have shared those struggles, then you can find women who have shared those same hard times and can help you find ways to move past them.

Keeping your struggles to yourself only allows them to fester inside of you until they become toxic for you and those around you.

Let it out lady, no matter how small. Breath it out into the world and set it free. Don't let your struggle become an unwanted squatter that becomes harder and harder to evict.

Part 3:

THE BOSS SIDE

B eing a Boss Mom is all about owning your passions and pursuing your dreams, but we all end up starting our businesses and families at different times and for different reasons. Each Boss Mom has a unique story about how they became a mother and an entrepreneur. The following women shared their stories about why they started their business and how that impacted their lives.

REASONS WE START BUSINESSES

Being a Boss Mom is the best of both worlds for me. When I became pregnant with my son, I thought for sure that I'd want to be a stay-at-home mom. We planned and shifted our finances so it could happen. When my expectations of being home full-time with my son didn't meet the day-to-day reality of the stay-at-home mom grind, I went back to work full-time.

Working full-time didn't work for me either, I missed too many special moments with my son and knew there had to be a way that I could have it all. I started my business because it seemed like the only way to have everything I wanted. I wanted to use my talents and passion to serve others and have a flexible schedule that allowed me still be home with my family.

Working for myself and remaining flexible to meet the needs

of my family is chaos most days. There are a lot of times when I have to work while they are around. The lessons my children are learning make it worth it. My son recently came home from school with a class fundraiser. He spent the afternoon in his room, writing a business plan and defining a target market. I couldn't have given him that exposure if I wasn't working on my business and raising my family at the same time.

– NJ Rongner

* * * *

I often get asked why I would choose to become a mom, start a business, and get my degree all at the same time. Well, I actually didn't really plan to do it all at the same time, it just happened that way.

I always knew that I wanted to earn a college degree. After high school I moved to Mexico to be a missionary. I started taking classes outside of work so that I could get my associates degree. A few years later I joined the military partially to help pay to finish my degree. I finally earned my associate degree and was on my way to my bachelor's degree when a friend asked me to help her brainstorm ways to grow her product-based business. We sat down and started to map out possible options, and something happened; I fell in love with business strategy. I went home, and I couldn't stop thinking about starting my own online business, so I did. Now keep in mind that in the midst of joining the military and taking college classes I managed to get married and have two children.

I juggled a lot. And I had to learn to give myself grace. There were days I'd be at work writing class assignments and blog posts, trying to finish both during my lunch hour.

I struggled with feeling guilty over the amount of time my husband spent watching the kids because I was working on homework or work. And I felt like I was putting him as a last priority, which is something I never wanted to do.

After six years in the U.S. Navy I decided it was time to make being a mom and an entrepreneur my top priorities. I was pregnant with our third child and we wanted to be closer to family so we moved back to Wisconsin where I grew up.

I know I have a lot going on in my life and I like it that way. I have learned how to be intentional about the choices I make. I can't do everything, and I have to be okay with it. I used to work a lot more, but with the recent announcement that we are expecting our fourth child, and running my own business, I have not been working as many hours per week. And that is an important lesson that less can be more, especially when you want to deliver quality work or make good grades.

If you are thinking about starting your own business and going to school on top of being a mom, then you need to establish boundaries. Learn that saying 'yes' means saying 'no' to something else. Your choices define who you are, the business you have and the relationships in your family. You can do it if you put your mind to it, even if it's one class at a time!

– Danielle Roberts

* * * *

It was the fall of 2012. My husband and I had just celebrated our one-year anniversary and were settled back into normal life after a whirlwind five-month trip backpacking around South America. I had spent the summer networking, applying for jobs, and interviewing while temping at my old job. Unfortunately, a Master's Degree in Education, six years' experience in the field, and stellar references didn't seem to be getting me very far.

To fill up my time, I worked on growing my Etsy shop that I had opened on a whim the month before leaving for the big adventure. I had always loved making things with my hands (especially jewelry), but it had always been a hobby. Now that I had nothing but time, in between coming up with new designs and starting a blog, I devoured whatever articles I could find on marketing, product photography, and selling at craft shows.

The more time passed, the less I wanted to return to a traditional job. My husband and I were just beginning to talk about having children, and I realized that I wanted to be home with my future family. I also knew that as much as I loved being around children, I would be bored if I didn't have something else. As the months passed, I came to accept that I had become what I had never imagined I would be: an entrepreneur. I fell in love with the idea of running my business while being a stay-at-home mom. I spent the next year working to grow my business, and in November 2013 I gave birth to my daughter. I was officially a Boss Mom.

The challenge came about six weeks after my daughter was born when I reopened my Etsy shop and started to get back in the groove of blogging. I had gone from working in my business for more than 40 hours per week to suddenly having to revolve my schedule around the needs of a baby with a very unpredictable routine. As someone who thrives on planning ahead, I found this very challenging. On any given day, I never knew what time or for how long I would be able to work. When my daughter was awake, I felt guilty if I wasn't interacting with her. I struggled to find a balance between attending to the needs of my daughter and fulfilling my needs as a business owner. I worried that I would never be able to devote the time I needed to work on my business and then felt crappy for feeling frustrated.

As my daughter got older and settled into a more predictable schedule, I felt the guilt fade away and my confidence as a Boss Mom increase. (Though, admittedly, it took many months to get there!) When she was four months old, I put my daughter in childcare two mornings a week so that I would have time to devote to my business. Of course, then I felt guilty that we were spending money on childcare when my business still had yet to turn a profit! I realized, though, that more than anything, I needed this for me.

Since then, we have found a mishmash of childcare solutions that work for our family and are affordable, from childcare swaps with other local moms, a parent-run co-op in our community, and having my mother-in-law watch her one day a week.

There have been many times over the years that I have felt overwhelmed and want to give up my business. What motivated me was knowing that I built something from the ground up that was absolutely mine. I love that my 3-year-old has a vague understanding of what I do. She knows that I make jewelry—and has even helped me with it—and write blog posts. And during those times where I feel on the brink of throwing it all the way, I give myself permission to take a vacation from my business.

My advice is to implement systems that will help you automate your business before your little one arrives. Those first few months after your baby is born will be a challenge and a big adjustment. The more you can hone in on what you want to do, work on attracting your ideal customers, and understand what is essential to running your business, the easier it will be to be to find a balance between being a stay-at-home and a work-at-home mom.

– Bev Feldman

* * * *

I know a ton of moms who started out as a stay-at-home mom and then decided later to start their own business. For me, I was a boss before I was a mom and it was harder than I thought to transition to motherhood.

I had been running my business since the age of 18 and almost a decade had gone by before I became a mom. The good news was I had always wanted to be a mom, and I built my business in a way that gave me flexibility and the freedom. Even though I run a brick and mortar business, I created systems and built a large team of about 40 people so that the business didn't need me there every day to keep it running.

I created a home office and decided to work exclusively from home before kids were ever on my radar. I was a little nervous I have to admit. I loved my business so much and was definitely a workaholic, and I wondered how I would be as a mom. I am one of those people that when I want something, I want it now, and when I decided to be a mom, unfortunately, things didn't go as planned.

My first pregnancy ended in a stillbirth when I was eight months pregnant, I was devastated, and it was followed by two miscarriages. Finally, my fourth pregnancy brought me my daughter. I took six months off to solely focus on being a mom and, during that time, I barely worked. My successful business was running without me, and it was a proud moment in my life. I was still bringing in income, but I was able to spend time with my little one.

When my daughter was six months old, I realized I was losing myself, my passion, and I wanted to get back to work. Finding a mix of being a mom and being a boss was more difficult than I expected. The mommy guilt was horrible. I first tried bringing in a nanny to our home. That failed miserably because whenever I took a call in my office, my daughter knew I was home and would bang on the office door. Then I decided to take her to daycare one day per week. I felt horribly guilty and a little embarrassed that my kid was going to daycare while I was at home. I wasn't getting enough done, and I think I was caring too much about what people thought about my situation. I had to let go of what other people thought and, more importantly, let go of the person inside my head telling me it was wrong to have my child in daycare.

Now I have two little ones, and they go to daycare three days per week and the other two days my husband, who works second shift, cares for them. I stopped feeling guilty when I realized how much my kids enjoyed making new friends and spending time with their dad, and that helps me know I am a good mom even when I am not with them while I work at home.

I finally found a better balance that works for my family and me. I am a work in progress, and as I change, the business changes and so does my family dynamic. At one point, my brick and mortar felt too easy, and I decided it was time for growth, so I added an online business to the mix of everything else I was doing. That threw a whole new set of challenges into our lives, but as a Boss Mom, you go where your heart and instinct take you.

No matter what your situation, do what is right for you and your family. That might be full-time daycare, that might be grandma watching them a few hours each day, or swapping services with another friend. The most important thing is that it works for you. Stop worrying what other people think, there are so many of us Boss Moms out there that are experiencing the same thing you are right now, and we absolutely get you and applaud you for pursuing your passions.

~ *Stacy Tuschl*

* * * *

Have you ever gone through your life working toward a goal or a dream, making sacrifices and doing all the right things, only to reach a point of achieving that goal or dream and having no clue what to do next? In 2015, that was me.

I'd been blissfully married for six years, welcomed my fourth daughter into the world and was literally living the exact life I'd envisioned for myself for years. Every day I got to wake up and pour the best of myself into raising my babies, loving my husband and running a home I was proud of. I was 25 years old, had already lived a lot of life and knew that I was in the exact season I was supposed to be in, doing exactly what I was supposed to be doing.

Honestly, I never would have predicted that one day I would have four kids. Growing up I wasn't much of a 'kid person,' I was ambitious and independent, with big dreams that kids (and maybe even marriage) didn't seem to align with. But when I met my husband, everything changed. Suddenly I found my former dreams replaced with dreams of nurturing a marriage, a family, and a home and it didn't take long after we got married for my baby fever to result in an actual baby. As much as I loved being married, being a mom felt like what I'd been made to do ... And I couldn't get enough!

From that point on, the number of kids wasn't ever really planned; I just never felt 'done.' We were open, life was generous, and our family grew until we reached four and we both knew our family was complete.

The biggest challenge with having four kids is feeling like there isn't enough time or 'you' to go around, and dealing with the frustration and guilt of feeling 'used up.' I want to give the best of myself and my time to each of my babies, and I can't always do that the way I want because there has to be enough of me to go around. I remember struggling in my later pregnancies with feeling like I was missing out on my older girls' early years because of being tired and struggling through various aspects of pregnancy. But you learn to push through that, savor what you can, embrace the imperfection of motherhood and accept the grace kids so freely give.And yet, one day a feeling of restlessness started creeping its way in. It was subtle at first, especially amidst the postpartum brain fog and daily chaos that was my life running a household and raising four girls ages five and under. But as the days ticked by, the feeling of "now what?" just wouldn't go away.

For years, I'd been pouring all of myself into building a family and proudly identifying myself as a wife and a mom and a homemaker—and I loved it! I truly felt fulfilled in what I was doing and took pride in the impact I was making.

But, I had a feeling deep inside that I was created for more. I wanted to make an even greater impact than I already was. I wanted to use the life and the gifts I'd been given to touch people's lives and make a difference. I wanted to create something that was truly mine, and I wanted it to be something that might help ease the weight of the financial hardships we were facing at the time.

What began as a feeling, grew into an idea which lead me to a precipice. I had a choice to make between doing the same thing day after day, ignoring that little feeling inside, or taking a leap of faith and taking a chance on myself and my dreams. I decided to go for it.

I'd always loved writing and helping people, so I settled on starting my very own blog where I would pour all of my life experience and expertise into inspiring wives and moms to join me in my pursuit of peaceful, purposeful, joyful living. The only problem was, I had zero experience writing a blog, no money to hire help, I was short on time and carrying around loads of self-doubt and preemptive guilt.

There were a million times I could have let all of those things stop me from moving forward with my dream. I was already a busy wife and mom with loads of responsibility on my plate. What if starting this new venture took away from that? What if I poured time and money into this and it made things harder instead of better for my family? Tons of questions like these were constantly swirling around in my head, but at the end of the day I decided to risk it. I decided that I needed to challenge myself to be willing to do this thing without having everything figured out, understanding that I would probably make mistakes, but that it also might actually be great.

The toughest thing about taking the plunge into life as a Boss Mom is definitely the guilt. Every choice you make, everything you do isn't about just you. There have been days that I am completely wracked with guilt, feeling like I will never be able to balance it all and that someone or something will always be getting the short end of the stick.

During the seasons that I'm wildly productive in my work, I often end up slacking in my marriage or spending time with my kids. When I'm focused and present in my home life and relationships, it can be really difficult to apply myself with the same tenacity in my work.

And the fact that I both live and work from my home doesn't make it any easier! I quickly learned that trying to juggle everything all the time, shouldering all the weight and all the guilt on my own doesn't work and will just make you crazy.

Instead, I've learned that you have to keep the big picture vision at the forefront of your mind at all times, while also taking everything one day at a time. I don't believe there is such a thing as balance in the life of a Boss Mom who is constantly switching back and forth between the many hats she wears. But, when you accept your limitations, own the areas where there is room for growth, learn how to partner with people and ask for help, and celebrate each little victory while embracing the progress in your process, Boss Mom life is better all around.

My advice is to be brave when it comes time to let go of the principles and ideals you've had in your head leading up to having kids. Take everything one step at a time, and be willing to do things you never thought you would in the name of living the best kind of reality for you and your family, not the one you spent years dreaming up in your head. You owe it to yourself and to your family to embrace the change and growth that will inevitably come every step of the way through your parenting journey. And don't let another day pass you by without taking a chance on yourself and on your dream.

- Kelsey Van Kirk

* * * *

What I love most about these stories are that each woman fell into being a Boss Mom in a different way. Some women are born to be Boss Moms, some dabble, and some are shoved into the entrepreneur and parenting world. Each path has led to amazing ideas and beautiful businesses. I hope that you know that your journey to becoming a Boss Mom is important and needs to be shared.

LOOKING FOR YOUR WHY

I remember someone telling me early on when I started my own business that, to succeed, I just had to find my why, find my purpose, I had to figure out what got me up in the morning. They made it seem so simple like it was just something you had to think through and it would come to you. So I put my head down and tried to figure out my 'why.'

But it didn't come to me. Sure, I had ideas. I wrote mission statements, came up with vision plans, and had major ah-ha moments, but it never truly took hold for me, or my audience. All the while, I was bombarded with people, articles, podcasts, and ads telling me the hot new tool and why it was going to be my ticket to success. I tried all sorts of techniques and bought all sorts of programs, but they never worked the way I expected.

I was determined to have a successful business, and I wanted it now. I wanted to wake up and know my 'why' and have that clarity everyone kept talking about. It took me a long time to realize that your 'why' is not something that jumps out at you in the beginning; it is something that reveals itself to you somewhere along the journey as you experiment and test out different methods to grow your business and ultimately, your life.

Looking back now, it took me two years to land on the Boss Mom brand and, in essence, my 'why.' It took me two years of testing, tweaking, and pivoting to discover my true passions and get to know myself enough on the business side to build my business up to a level of financial viability. It felt so long at the time, but now I see how brief a time it was and how necessary a lot of that time and learning was to get me to where I am now.

During that time, I felt guilty, sad, worthless, uncertain, and often, a failure. I was so sure I was meant to have my own business, and I had such big dreams that I constantly questioned whether my determination was misguided and would end up leading me, and my family, down a path of despair. I know it sounds melodramatic, but when you put everything on the line to prove that you can build something on your own, you feel the invisible weight of the world on your shoulders, and it feels pretty heavy at times.

I remember looking at other entrepreneurs that looked like they were killing it and wondering why it wasn't working for me; that maybe I wasn't as 'fortunate' as those women. If I had known that so many other female entrepreneurs experienced similar self-doubt, I might not have felt so alone and scared.

We all know that it can be hard to find that one true love in your life, so why do we think that finding our one true purpose will be an easier? The fact is that you have to get out and experience life to find your purpose. You gain clarity in the creation process itself. We don't find the love of our life by sitting at home writing out lists of what we want. Sure, that is a great starting point, and we should always take the time to map out what we know we want and don't want in our lives, but after that, you have to go out into the world.

The best way to find that one love is to start doing more of the things you love. If you love to run, join a running club. If you love to paint, take painting classes. Suddenly, you will start to connect with people that love the same things you do. Over time, you stop thinking your goal is to meet someone, and your goal becomes creating more wonderful experiences, and that is when the magic happens.

The catch 22 is that you have to give all of your ideas a chance so that you can see which one really lights you up long term. Every time you say "I just had a breakthrough," or "It finally came to me," I want you to love that idea with all of your heart and give it the chance it deserves until it either becomes so clear that you are meant to be forever, or that it's time to let go.

You are no less of an entrepreneur when you have ideas that don't bear fruit. No one ever asks you how many people you dated before you met your partner and judges you for the relationships that didn't work before the one that did. If you want to feel confident about your direction, then **find other women who are on different points in their path so that you can learn from those ahead of you, connect with those beside you, and teach those behind you.** Be more concerned with surrounding yourself with people who bring out the best in you, and your 'why' will reveal itself. It might take some time, but if you let yourself, you will have one heck of a ride along the way.

Pursuing Balance

Ah the elusive balance, the notion that everything feels as though everything holds equal value in your life and all is calm and as it should be. It's all a bunch of bull honky. Pursuing balance is exhausting, guilt-ridden, and just plain no fun.

Balance seems so hard to pursue and so difficult to attain because it is. Rarely is anything equal in our lives and that's ok. Oprah said, "you can have it all, just not all at once" and she was right. You can be an amazing mom, entrepreneur, wife, daughter, friend, but rarely at the same time. Once again, that's ok. No one expects you to be perfect all the time, they expect you to be there when they really need you, and that is where the real challenge comes into play.

We experience a constant tug in priorities that make us feel out of balance because we perceive that everyone needs us all the time, but we are wrong. I know, the idea is hard to swallow for some of us. Whether we want to admit it or not, we often WANT to be needed, even if it feels overwhelming and we complain about it all the time, which I am guilty of doing.

If you want to feel a sense of harmony in your life, then you need to start owning your decisions. This is easier said than done, so if you are shaking your head right now, I understand. We all experience guilt because we question our decisions. We often question ourselves and care about what other's might think, even if we don't admit it. **I do believe that you can become confident in your decisions and allow any negative energy that comes your way to move past you quickly, and it all starts with knowing your priorities.**

First things first, write down your deal breakers. This will help you say no, even when something looks alluring, but doesn't align. For example, I love to speak, and I ultimately want to travel more and speak, but a deal breaker I established when I had my daughter was that I did not want to be away for more than three days and no more than twice a month. This means that when I am offered a spot to speak, I have to evaluate the timing to make sure it doesn't meet any of my deal breaker criteria. This makes saying no a lot easier than it would have been without mapping out my deal breakers. Of course, I am always able to make exceptions because I am the boss and I am able to determine if the benefits outweigh my deal breaker criteria.

After you know your deal breakers, write down times when you know certain parts of your life will take the front seat. Maybe it's when you are at the end of a large project, or the kids' birthdays, or that annual vacation. These help you set your calendar so that you aren't forced to make difficult decisions as often.

Now, write out your drop everything list. This might be if your kid goes to the hospital, one particular large client has an urgent need, a close friend unexpectedly comes to town, or your favorite store has a surprise flash sale. Yep, that's right, your drop everything list doesn't always have to be the standard list that everyone expects, it just needs to reflect what's most important to you. This will help you either say no or accept support in situations where priorities conflict.

For instance, if I am in the middle of a live product launch and one of my children gets a fever, I let my family know I will need help. I make sure I have a backup plan. My business takes a front seat during a launch. When I am business as usual, then when someone gets sent home with a fever, they take priority. Knowing what takes priority when, will help me plan, and not feel so bad about my decisions.

This method has helped me get rid of guilt and be more open with my community about my priorities, which has made me realize that there are so many women out there struggling with the same guilt and lack of decision-making confidence that I sometimes have. Map out your deal breakers and your priorities and watch the guilt melt away. It will want to creep back in, so post your priorities on the wall so that your guilt knows it's no longer invited to the party.

COLLABORATION OVER COMPETITION

There is a new wave of thinking. I didn't start the revolution, but I am sure going to ride the wave. The idea that to succeed we must do better than our competitors is no longer the mindset of the day. **Entrepreneurs everywhere are starting to realize that success is not achieved by exclusion, but rather by inclusion.**

It reminds me of the movie Chocolat from 2000. The movie takes place in an old French village (which I have actually visited by the way) where a nomad chocolatier and her daughter open up a chocolate shop. The mayor of the town sees the chocolatier as an indulgent threat to his small religious town. The mayor's tactic is to start a ban on her shop, while her plan is to befriend everyone and help solve their problems. Of course, there are times when it feels as though the mayor has the upper hand, but ultimately collaboration wins the day. The mayor's version of community is all based on negativity and judgment, while the chocolatier's method is to ask questions, listen, and engage. It is beautiful to watch as each character unfolds through their stories. At the end, even the mayor is transformed, and the village unites in celebration.

So the question is whether you want to fester over in a corner, or whether you want to hold a celebration. Competition is all about leaving others behind, while collaboration is all about raising everyone up around us.

Sometimes we keep ourselves from wonderful collaborations because we get scared that if we befriend our competitors, we will lose business, and that might be true, in fact, you might even send business their way. But I will tell you now that there is more than enough people and money to go around. Besides, very rarely do we have direct competitors that are like us in every way.

Think of it this way, if you were to clone two babies, then the only time they would ever be exactly the same would be the moment they were born. From that moment on they would have different experiences, and as time went on would become more and more different and unique. If even clones are unique, then so are you.

When we think about competition this way, then we stop trying to understand our unique advantages through our products and services and realize that our unique advantage lies in how we build our brand, and what we stand for.

I am by no means the only content strategist out there. I am not even the only content strategist for mom entrepreneurs. My strength is in who I am and what I bring to the table because of my unique story. The Boss Mom brand, which is really an extension of me, is funny, playful, and loves a good relationship analogy. I'm terrible at keeping secrets, especially my own, and think that sharing more than is usually comfortable is an absolute requirement. Women and men hire me because they need a content strategist and they resonate with these characteristics.

And when we don't get each other's jokes I refer them to other content strategists that might be a better fit. If I thought of other content strategists as competitors, then I would have no one to recommend, and I would only be able to send people away, instead of adding value by connecting people. I actually strengthen my brand by being honest about who my ideal client is, and being open to help connect people to the right tools for their unique path. It's a win, win process.

Don't get me wrong, not all people are open and willing, and not all people are nice or even good business owners. I don't connect and collaborate with everyone. I use my gut and their story to help me decide if it is a good idea to collaborate, but I never let the worry of competition get it in the way.

Part 4:

FINDING YOUR TRIBE

W e all need a tribe, and if you feel like you are surrounded by people that don't get you, then you have not found your tribe yet. In fact, I think we need many tribes throughout our lifetime.

Your tribe is not only those people that get you; but they are also the people that will surround you when danger arises and protect you, even when you didn't ask to be protected. They will assume roles in your life that will fulfill you in ways you didn't realize were needed.

Your tribe is about so much more than finding friends; a tribe is all about a sense of belonging. **When you have a tribe, you feel at home and accepted.** When you have a tribe, you open up and engage more than you thought you would. When you have a tribe, you engage with empathy instead of just sympathy because you understand each other.

We should all seek to be a part of a tribe, but to find a tribe we must be willing to be vulnerable, and that is often the most challenging part, but it doesn't have to be.

Who Will "Get Me"?

How do you know who will make you feel at home? When you feel alone it is hard to imagine that there are people out there who will make you feel better, but they are out there and they are waiting for you.

First, think about what you love to talk about but feel like no one you currently know is interested in the topic. I noticed that talking about owning a business around women who had jobs or stayed at home wasn't a very fun conversation. Not for them and not for me. There was nothing wrong with my friends; they were amazing people, they just didn't care about building an online brand, or the latest online tool. I recognized that there was a topic I was interested in sharing and I needed to find other women who cared about those topics too.

Next, don't stop at one topic, make sure to really brainstorm until you feel like you have nothing left to say, and then keep going. Brainstorming should feel uncomfortable, that's how you know it's working. Break down the topics into smaller topics. For instance, I knew I wanted to be around mom entrepreneurs, but I also knew I wanted them to identify as creative entrepreneurs. I knew that I loved to talk about business strategy, process, and tools, so I knew that I wanted to find people that talked more about business than the parenting side.

And finally, once you have a list, prioritize them by the topics that are most important to you, so you know where to start. This list will provide you with the keywords you need to find your groups either online through Facebook and LinkedIn, or in person through Meetups and other live events.

The reason it's a good idea to brainstorm lots of topics is that it may take time to find the group that makes you come alive. Don't settle, if a group of ladies doesn't make you feel loved and supported and happy, then move on to another group. Your perfect tribe is out there and the longer you hang around people that don't make you feel at home, the more opportunity for you to question your value. Don't wait, start looking for your tribe now.

Where to Look

Your tribe could be anywhere, so where do you look? Well, let's start with places where groups of people connect that might like the same things you like. This might be online or in person; both are great ways to connect.

Facebook groups and LinkedIn groups are great places to start because you don't even need to shower or get out of your pajamas to participate. These groups are searchable and specific, so you can simply search for words that matter to you and immediately find pre-built communities full of people that all care about that one particular topic. If you want to find other mom entrepreneurs and you do a search on Facebook, you will find tons of groups that are full of other mom entrepreneurs. There are thousands of groups on both platforms full of amazing people who all love different things, and they have self-curated themselves into groups just for you.

The Boss Mom group is a vibrant group of amazing women, and it might be just right for you, but it might not. The only way to know is to try out other groups too. So here is how you find the right group or groups for you.

1. Pick a few keywords that describe the kind of people you are looking for and do a search on Facebook or LinkedIn (try the platform you already hang out in most frequently).

2. Read the description in the sidebar of each group to decide whether it's the right group for you (don't worry we will narrow it

down later).

3. Pick three to five groups that sound like a fit and ask to join. If they take more than a week to accept you into the group then put them at the bottom of your list, you are going to prefer a group where the admins are engaged.

4. For the next week, plan to spend thirty minutes several days a week, more if you want, in these groups. About 7-10 minutes in each group will give you a good assessment. If you find a group that just pulls you in then you know you have a winner, but give the other groups a chance.

5. You might be tempted to lurk around the group and take all of the information in but never comment or post. I am here to challenge you to post at least two times in each group to see what happens. Post a question or a challenge you are currently facing, do not promote your business, simply ask for support and see if you get it.

6. At the end of the week, gauge which groups you felt the most connection and stay in those groups. Leave the groups that didn't work.

7. Follow this process for any other types of groups you want to join. It does take a little bit of research and time, but then you can be confident you have found a good place that is worth your time in the future.

Make sure you aren't discouraged by the size of the groups you find. Small groups might not seem popular, but don't judge too fast, maybe they are just starting, and you will be there from the beginning, or maybe they like staying small to stay more intimate. And don't discount larger groups either. You can absolutely find your tribe in a big group. Think about your high school, college, or workplace; they probably had a large group of people, but you were still able to meet individuals in your classes or after-hours activities. It is easier to find a connection in a large virtual group than you might think. You won't get to know everyone, and you don't need to. You will find your group of people, and they will find you. The Boss Mom group is getting rather large and is still amazing and intimate in a lot of ways.

If online isn't quite right for you, then check out an in-person Meetup or attend a live event. These days people are giving you so much information about who they are and what they like, which makes it easier than ever to find the right group for you. The first step is to put yourself out there and to be open to meeting new people and creating new experiences.

How to Engage

Don't be a lurker. Spending time in online communities and never saying anything is like sitting in the corner at a dance and watching everyone else have fun. Go out and make new friends and memories. I know that engaging means you have to be willing to be a little bit vulnerable, I get it. You might be sitting there saying to yourself, "what if no one wants to connect with me?" I am here to tell you that there are people who want to be your new business bestie or mom support circle.

Once you find a community, or communities, that you love, you want to get to work connecting with others in the group. **You might think that the best way to connect is to introduce yourself, but I say listen first, and then seek to be heard second.** Start by looking at existing conversations and offer comments and support. Adding comments, expertise, and support helps give you a sense of how the rest of the community interacts and what kinds of posts get the best interaction. This is also a time to see if any particular people stand out to you. Maybe you notice someone posting about a current challenge that resonates with you because you are dealing with the same thing, or had that experience in the past. Maybe you just like the ideas and personality of one particular person in the group. These observations will help you find your 'people' quicker.

Remember when I said not to be a lurker? If you spend your time reading posts and comments but never participate, you will begin to find your people, but as time passes you will know those people more, and they will still have no idea who you are. It is much harder to start a relationship when they don't know you exist . . . So engage. Once you have spent some time offering support and expertise, then you can start to post. This process doesn't have to take more than a week so don't feel like you have to wait months before you can post. This is not a playbook with absolute rules. Just like with dating, if you want to post that first day because you have a question, then go ahead. You don't have to wait three days to call someone you like, just do it. If you aren't sure what to do then follow this process, but listen to your gut, it is usually right.

When it comes to posts in online communities you have to remember that posts are a lot like jokes, not all of them are going to be funny. If you post something in a community and it's like crickets, don't get discouraged, there are a lot of factors at play in any online community. I suggest asking a question or telling a story and at the end ask who can relate.

The one thing you should NOT do is try to teach people when

they don't ask for it. I know you have amazing value and that you want to share it, but a big long post aimed at teaching you a life lesson very rarely creates great engagement. Instead, create questions that get people to share their stories so you can see who might need your help and then engage with those people on a more personal level. You will be amazed at how you are able to find your ideal client and future friends when you engage this way.

Now if you are looking to simply connect on a mom level then I still think asking questions and telling stories is the best way to go. I posted a lot about my struggles with potty training my son and his crazy trauma with pooping. I remember getting a book from my brother, who had a really easy time potty training his son, and the first page of the book basically said, "if you have ever said that your child is not ready to be potty trained, then you are not a dedicated parent." I immediately threw the book away and jumped into the Boss Mom group and told everyone my situation and asked for women who experienced something similar. My brother had the best intentions, but our experiences were different, and that book made me feel like a terrible parent, even though that was not true. In fact, I think the author of the book had noble intentions, but her experience was not my experience so I went out and found my potty trauma besties and they helped me get my son to poop regularly. Boy, am I glad we are over that hump!

The important point about engaging with groups and finding your people is that everyone supports everyone. **We don't just wait until times are bad to ask for help, we seek out those that need to be supported when we have the space to offer help.** A community is a place where everyone pulls their weight. It is not always equal and if you have to bow out sometimes or decide that the community is no longer for you then don't feel guilty about leaving or taking time off, your community will be there for you when you feel it's the right time to return.

If You Can't Find It, Start It

If you find yourself in the unfortunate predicament where no community fits your needs, then you must boldly step up and create your own group. Of course, you have a choice. **You can decide to sit there and feel alone, or you can decide to be the beacon that shines bright and calls out to all the other women who wish they had a support system.**

Starting your own group might sound scary, and I am not going to tell you that it will be all rainbows and rose petals, but it is totally worth the effort and I will tell you why. This world is full of amazing people that have not reached their full potential because they are scared to step out into the world and be themselves. These amazing people are scared to be themselves because they are worried that other people will judge them for who they are and what they love. In many cases, they are right, people will judge them and call them 'weird' or some other trending word. **I can't change that the world isn't perfect, but I can tell you that creating a space where people can come together and feel connected and at home is the answer to freedom.**

If you are looking for a community and can't find it, then I bet you other people are looking for that same kind of community too. **Imagine how many wonderful people you could help open up and flourish because you decided to create a place where they can feel at home and understood.** Imagine how many wonderful ideas, relationships, and lives you can impact because you decided to create a place where people felt supported and loved.

So many people look at places like Facebook and see a fun platform to post pictures and funny memes, but I see a place where lives are changed. I see a place where we can find our people, become who we are meant to be, and help others find their path too. If you see what I see, then you are meant to create your own community, and I truly hope that you do.

Part 5:

THE TRUE CONFESSION

BISCUITS & TEA

The country singer Kacey Musgraves put out a brilliant album called Pageant Material in 2015. What I love most about Kacey is that she just wants us all to embrace who we are and stop judging each other. This idea is playfully brought out in all of her songs, but two, in particular, spoke to me and the essence of the Boss Mom Movement. Her song "Biscuits" is all about living our own lives and letting others live theirs. She talks about mending your own fences and taking care of your own business (which she refers to as biscuits) and life will be 'gravy'. I smile every time I hear it. The song also shines a light on the idea that we are all just people trying to live our lives and that judging each other and making other people feel unloved doesn't help anyone.

She goes on to sing a wonderful line about not understanding the journeys others are on, so just be YOU and I'll be ME. This is exactly the kind of Boss Mom confession I want everyone to know and embrace. Until you know everything about someone, which is pretty near impossible, you can't truly understand what they are experiencing or why they make certain choices in their life. **I am not here on Earth to spend my time trying to figure out why people did things that don't make sense to me. It's a waste of energy. Instead, I want to spend my time getting to know myself and finding other people who like who I am.**

In another Kasey Musgraves song called 'Cup of Tea' she says (paraphrased here) - everyone likes their tea differently - some hot, some cold. You can't be the perfect fit for everyone. The idea behind these lyrics are simple and yet so powerful, and speaks to another Boss Mom Confession: **Not everyone is going to like me, and that doesn't bother me because the only way I can find my true tribe is to be vocal about what is important to me.** The moment I really embraced this idea was the moment things started falling into place for my business and my life. I used to hold my ideas and passions in because I was worried that people might not like them, but I didn't stop to think about the fact that other people might love my ideas. I let the possible negatives mask over the possible positives, and I spent years of my life only letting half of my true self out into the world. I will tell you right now that I wasn't doing anyone any favors by not owning my own crazy. When I finally decided to let my silly singing, spontaneous dancing, dating referencing self out into the world something amazing happened. I started making friends who would sing right back, and groups of women who would dance right there with me. I began to see women open up and let their fun quirky personality out into the world and I fell in love. I fell in love with each one of those women who were so different from me, but yet the same. I fell in love with all of the amazing ideas and connection that started to happen when we let our true selves out into the world, and this all came about because I decided that I wasn't interested in making everyone happy. **I decided to dedicate myself to two things: Allowing myself to be happy, and accepting that everyone else is just trying to do the same thing.** As you go through life, I encourage you to live by this motto of biscuits and tea. Stop trying to please everyone, just be yourself, and life will be gravy.

CIRCLES OF UNDERSTANDING

Have you ever asked for advice about your business from a person you love when you knew they didn't really understand what you do? Maybe you wanted to find out if a particular product idea was viable and you asked your mom what she thought, but she has never started a business, and she has no idea what an online business looks like. She gives you the best advice she can give, and you end up going home completely deflated because she wasn't half as excited about the idea as you were. If you really thought about it, do you think that your mom was the best person to ask?

I used to do it all the time. I would assume that my close circle of influence in my life would give me the right kind of advice on all possible topics, but that doesn't make sense at all. Just like you can't find a master virtual assistant that does everything you could ever need, there is no one person that will always have the right kind of advice no matter what family or business topic you throw their way. We are meant to have a circle of influence, but it also means we need to know our circle of understanding too.

Here is how it works. Draw a circle with a dot in the middle and then create equal pie pieces for the main areas where you usually seek advice. For me, I have business, parenting, spiritual, marriage, womanhood, and adventure. These are the parts of my life where I want to make sure I find the right people that understand that part of my life to offer the right kind of help. Once you have your pie pieces named, then you list out the main people in your life and decide where they go in your circle chart. The center of the circle represents a true understanding of the topic, and you, and the outskirts of the circle mean they have no interest or knowledge on that topic. So your partner might be close to the center in the parenting category, and your mom might be close to the center for the womanhood category, but they both aren't even on the radar in the business section. Now that you have everyone close to you plotted out on your Circle of Understanding chart you can go about your life per usual. The moment you feel like you need support and advice on a particular topic, go to your chart and see who is closest to the center in that category. This person, or set of people, are the ones you should go to for help. These people will get excited about your ideas, challenge you in the right ways, and ultimately give advice you respect because you know they understand that particular topic.

The true confession here is that just because I love you doesn't mean I expect you to have great advice about everything in my life. And I realize now that putting the burden on the people I love to give me good advice on topics they don't understand or care to understand, is unfair of me. We can all live happier lives when we know our Circles of Understanding so uncover yours.

STOP BEING EMBARRASSED

Did you know that I didn't buy a Lotto ticket for years because I didn't know the correct process and I was embarrassed to ask? Of course, you didn't know because my husband is the only one, until now, that was privy to that little ridiculous fact. Sadly, it is totally true. I was too embarrassed to ask a complete stranger that I would never see again how you buy a Lotto ticket so I just never bought one. And I was too embarrassed that my friends would think I was dumb for not knowing so I never said anything. I could be a millionaire right now if wasn't so embarrassed that I would look stupid for being an adult that didn't know how the process worked. And, once I figured out how it works, to this day my heart starts pumping when I go to buy a ticket—and it's not because I'm excited about winning. This example just goes to show you how feeling embarrassed can keep us from the simplest of tasks and often keeps us from doing powerful and impactful things in our lives.

Here's another example that I still have trouble with all of the time. I am embarrassed to be sexy. When I got out of college and moved back to San Diego, I was sending out my mock-up news reel to small stations across the U.S. trying to find a job. Actually, who am I kidding, I knew I didn't really want to be a news anchor anymore, so I wasn't trying very hard. It was no surprise that I didn't get any job offers. I went back to being a cocktail waitress at the Brigantine restaurant by the Del Mar racetrack until I could figure out what I wanted to do. I met a guy who came into the restaurant often, and we started dating. He got me a part-time job writing synopsis' for old movies and shows they were converting to DVD . . . you know the ones you see at Target in the dollar section. I loved that job. At that time, I was 22 and had no idea what one wears at a real job, so I wore cute skirts and acted 22 because that was all I knew how to do. Needless to say, no one took me very seriously, which is funny because that job is where I discovered I was meant to be an entrepreneur, but that's a story for another time. The point is that it burned an idea into my subconscious that told me that if I were sexy in any way, I would not be able to advance in my career.

Now, on the surface that might not be a bad mentality to have, but it spread into all areas of my life. As I got older, I started covering everything up and became very self-conscious about how I looked and what that said about me. I wonder if it was ever something anyone on the outside ever noticed, but I always grappled with what I wore and felt embarrassed that maybe I was not portraying the right 'me' in the right places. That all changed in 2014. I had gone back to the Midwest and ended up living in Columbus, Ohio with my husband. Once we had our son I wanted to move back to San Diego to be closer to my family and my husband was happy to comply. I ended up getting invited to a women's networking event that took place in the evening. I remember seeing a woman with a gorgeous dress that was low cut in the front and low cut in the back and was showing all sorts of skin. She was beautiful and sexy, and she was flaunting it all over the place. I kept wondering what on earth she was thinking wearing that to this event until my inner voice was interrupted by the announcement that the main sponsor for the night was *Scripps Clinic* and that their chief surgeon was there to give a short talk. Sure enough, the woman in that sexy dress walked up to the stage. My entire world changed that night. I saw a woman who had embraced her femininity in every way and didn't let it stop her from also being smart and respected.

I might never wear that kind of dress to an event, but **I am no longer embarrassed to be a sexy woman, and that is my confession.** I have boobs and curves, and I can flaunt them if I want. I don't care that I had two babies and that I don't have the same body I had when I was 22. I don't care if people think I should dress a certain way because I am a mom or a certain age or in a certain profession. Sometimes I wear pajamas and a hoodie, and sometimes I wear four-inch heels and I feel great both ways.

I think we should all allow ourselves to feel and be sexy. A good friend of mine, Jen Rozenbaum, started the Shamelessly Feminine movement and I just love everything she stands for. I think that allowing ourselves to be sexy is one of the first things we let go of when we become moms. And I am not talking about being sexy for someone else; I am talking being sexy for you. So go put on that one outfit you stopped wearing because you were embarrassed that a mom shouldn't wear that and just strut your stuff. We all deserve to feel sexy, and I think you should start right now.

I WANT TO LIVE IN A WORLD WHERE . . .

When we wake up in the morning, we have a choice. We can either choose to see how messed up the world is, or we can choose to see how much opportunity there is in the world. I like how Helen Keller put it, "Life is either a daring adventure or nothing at all."

Each of us gets to choose our own adventure, and each of us is presented with crazy challenges that throw us off course or bring us to a standstill. I want to live in a world where no person feels like they have to go through these challenges alone. **I want to live in a world where we spend more time supporting and connecting with other people than worrying about what people think about us.** I want to live in a world where no one is afraid to share their story, and everyone embraces each other's stories even if we don't understand them.

I feel like this place is starting to exist and I am so honored to be a part of this new world. I confess that I am not always the beacon of light in all of these areas, but I am always working to improve and grow. Anytime I feel like I have been thrown off track I go back to my tribe, and I confess how I feel and where I'm at and they always band around me with support and love. That moment when I stop listening to myself, and I let people into my life that make me feel bad or sad about myself I stop for a moment and ask myself who has control over my world and the answer is always me. It isn't always easy, but in the end, my happiness is important and so is yours, so don't ever feel guilty about doing what is right for you and your family.

Right now, you live in a world where there are thousands of Boss Moms who want you to know that you are not alone. Your tribe is out there waiting for you, so what are you going to do today to find your people and let your crazy shine?

Part 6:
WHAT'S NEXT . . .

The Boss Mom Tribe

If you don't already have a tribe of mom entrepreneurs in your corner, then we would love for you to join our Boss Mom community. If this book resonated with you, then you will love all of the amazing women in our group. We are all about brainstorming, supporting, challenging, and collaborating to help each other's businesses move forward. Our community is about nurturing and raising each other up so that we can all succeed and feel fulfilled in all aspects of our lives.

Join us at **www.boss-mom.com/join** and get access to a great resource and an amazing community of women.

The Boss Mom Companion

If you aren't sure how to find your tribe, then we have something that might help. We want to make sure you feel connected and supported, and we realize that there are tons of communities out there that might be the perfect fit for you, so we compiled a list of communities and resources for different kinds of journeys. The Boss Mom Companion is a free resource guide and course that not only helps you find your people but also goes more in depth on how to engage in different communities so that you can get past any fear or doubt and start to get the support you want and need. You are not alone, and we want you to know that's true as soon as possible.

All you have to do is go to **www.boss-mom.com/bmc** and you can get instant access to the Boss Mom Companion for free. Don't wait another minute to get your companion and stop feeling alone.

About the Author

Dana is a mother to two amazing kids who don't care what 'normal' means and is married to a Commercial Banker who loves to invent new words to popular songs. She started the Boss Mom Movement back in 2015 after dealing with the guilt of not wanting to be a stay-at-home mom, which led to her writing the first Boss Mom book. With two kids in tow, within a year, she was able to grow Boss Mom into a vibrant community and business. She embraces the days when she needs to cry and happily opens up to her tribe so that she can get the support she needs without guilt. Dana wakes up every morning and gets excited to build tents with her kids and then send them off to school so she can work on content strategy with her clients. She is a constant work in progress and made a pact with herself that she would never let guilt or embarrassment keep her from being true to herself.

Acknowledgements

Thank you to all of the wonderful contributors to this book; you are changing lives by sharing your story, and I am eternally grateful. To Liz Thompson, my amazing editor and friend, you have a beautiful and voracious mind, and I am so incredibly honored to have you in my life. I can't wait for the day when you write your book and unleash it on the world. To CJ Thomas who has been with me since the beginning documenting this journey through photos. I am honored that I've had the opportunity to see you flourish and grow in your craft; you are a friend and a joy to this world. To Lilah Higgins, you bring my dreams to life, and I am grateful every day that you are who you are. To Alexa Bigwarfe, who's resilience is a light for all women, I hope you wake up one morning in the near future covered in ladybugs.

To my parents, my husband, and my children, you are the beacon that keeps me from crashing into the sea, and I cannot imagine a world without you in it.

To Dawn Marrs, Kelsey Murphy, Natalie Gingrich, NJ Rongner, Danielle Roberts, Kelsey Van Kirk, Valerie Friedlander, Natalie Hughes, Veronica Staudt, and so many others in the Boss Mom community, you have impacted my life in ways that I can't even express with words. Thank you.

And to you, Boss Mom, thank you for being open and vulnerable. Your voice and your story are important, and you are creating a better world. Thank you for having a beautiful heart.

Contributors

Alexa Bigwarfe, Write.Publish.Sell, Author Coach and Publisher
http://writepublishsell.co
Bev Feldman, Linkouture, Chief Creative Officer
https://www.linkouture.com
Carrie Wood, More Love Mama Global Textiles
http://www.morelovemama.etsy.com
Celeste Coffman, Thoughtful Journey Counseling, CEO and
Therapist
http://www.CelesteCoffman.com
Danielle Roberts, Legacy Creative Company, Business Manager
and Strategist
http://legacycreativeco.com
Elizabeth Thompson, House Style Editing
http://housestyleediting.com
Jen Rozenbaum, Jen Rozenbaum/ShamelesslyFeminine
http://www.jenrozenbaum.com
Kelsey Van Kirk, Simply, Life on Purpose
http://www.kelseyvankirk.com
Laurie Joy, The Mojo Mama
http://themojomama.com
Marietta Goldman, Marietta Goldman Group LLC
http://www.mariettagoldman.com
Monica Froese, Redefining Mom LLC, Business Strategist
https://redefiningmom.com

Monika Jefferson, DTH public Relations, Public Relations Strategist, Entrepreneur and speaker
http://www.monijeffersonpr.com

Natalie Gingrich, More Mom Movement
http://moremommovement.com

NJ Rongner, Digital Marketing Consultant
http://www.willowandanchor.com

Nicole Hoglund, Honestly Able, Confidence Coach for Entrepreneurs & Executives
http://honestlyable.com

Samantha Johnston, Neapolitan Creative
http://neapolitancreative.com

Stacy Tuschl, She's Building Her Empire - Marketing strategist and high-performance coach
http://www.shesbuildingherempire.com

Tara Bosler, T. Bosler Writing
http://www.tboslerwriting.com

Val Breit, The Common Cents Club and Keep Calm Write On, Entrepreneur, Author & Editor
http://www.TheCommonCentsClub.com and
http://www.KeepCalmWriteOn.com